Gravure
Primer

by Cheryl L. Kasunich

GATF*Press*
Pittsburgh

International Standard Book Number: 0-88362-205-X
Library of Congress Catalog Card Number: 97-74135

Printed in the United States of America
GATF Catalog No. 1329

Printed on Williamsburg Offset, 60 lb., Smooth Finish

GATF*Press*
Graphic Arts Technical Foundation
200 Deer Run Road
Sewickley, PA 15143-2600
Phone: 412/741-6860
Fax: 412/741-2311
Email: info@gatf.org
Internet: http://www.gatf.org

TABLE OF CONTENTS

FOREWORD

A crash course in gravure printing? Yes, that's what we have asked of Cheryl L. Kasunich, executive vice president of the Gravure Association of America and a twenty-year veteran of the gravure industry. Though the history of gravure printing dates back more than two centuries, this book offers a short, illustrated, non-technical orientation to the field along with a glossary of basic terms.

The aim of the GATF*Press* primer series is to communicate the essential concepts of printing processes and technologies. Other primers focus on lithography, flexography, and screen printing, and new titles are being planned.

Gravure Primer is useful to students, graphic artists, print buyers, publishers, salespeople in the graphic communications industry— to anyone who would like to know more about the printing process.

GATF*Press* is committed to serving the graphic communications community as a leading publisher of technical information. Please visit the GATF website at http://www.gatf.org for additional information about our resources and services.

Peter Oresick
Director
GATF*Press*

PREFACE

For more than 50 years the Gravure Association of America (GAA) has provided support and technical publications for the gravure industry. The gravure process itself predates the current commercial printing processes. The simplicity of gravure printing has made it easy to automate. Over the years, gravure has been able to incorporate emerging technologies to continually improve the process.

This book is the first primer published on the gravure process, and was written for individuals with a basic understanding of print reproduction who want to learn about gravure. I hope that it provides the fundamentals of the gravure process for practitioners, print and packaging buyers, designers, advertisers, and students. As an introductory reference it also covers the gravure markets, mechanical principles, and image carrier manufacturing. References to standards and a glossary of gravure related terminology are also included.

I am grateful to the Graphic Arts Technical Foundation for the opportunity to provide this information to a wider audience. Its interest in this project is to be commended. Much of the information in this primer has been derived from GAA technical publications and the textbook *Gravure: Process and Technology*. I owe special thanks to all the individuals who have contributed their knowledge for the advancement of the gravure industry.

Cheryl L. Kasunich
Gravure Association of America

1200A Scottsville Road
Rochester, NY 14624
Phone: 716/436-2150
Fax: 716/436-7689
Internet: http://www.gaa.org

1 THE PRINTING PROCESSES

Printing may be defined as the reproduction of images affixed to a physically permanent substrate (as opposed to a television screen or computer monitor) in quantities of one or more. The term substrate literally means "the layer beneath" and may be used to express any printed surface, whether it be paper, foil, metal, glass, wood, or cloth. The act of printing requires an image carrier to transfer the image to a substrate. Any two-dimensional image can be defined as having an image area and a nonimage area. These two distinct areas must be separated on an image carrier. Each of the printing principles described below varies in how the image and nonimage areas are kept distinct from one another. This book provides an in-depth explanation of only the gravure printing process.

GRAVURE

Gravure is an intaglio printing process. The image carrier has the image cut or etched below the surface of the nonimage area (Figure 1-1). On the gravure image carrier, all the images are screened creating thousands of tiny cells.

During printing, the image carrier is immersed in fluid ink. As the image carrier rotates, ink fills the tiny cells and covers the surface of the cylinder. The surface of the cylinder is wiped with a doctor blade, leaving the nonimage area clean while the ink remains in the recessed cells. Substrate is brought into contact with the image carrier with the help of an impression roll. At the point of contact, ink is drawn out of the cells onto the substrate by capillary action.

Gravure is used for publications, catalogs, Sunday newspaper supplements, labels, cartons, flexible packaging, gift wrap, wall and floor coverings, and a variety of precision coating applications.

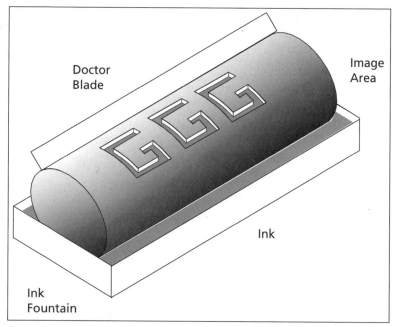

Figure 1-1. Rotogravure image carriers are engraved, either chemically or mechanically, so that the image areas are recessed.

FLEXOGRAPHY

Flexography is a rapidly-growing printing process that is used mainly in the packaging and newspaper printing segments of the graphic arts industry. The process is well suited for printing on foils and other types of nonabsorbent substrates. The principle of image transfer involves an image area that is physically raised above a non-image area (Figure 1-2). This is the principle referred to as relief printing. The image area comes into contact with an inked roller, and the nonimage area, being lower than the image area, does not get inked. An impression roller forces that substrate against the relief image and thus an image is formed.

The process is called flexography because the image carrier, or flexographic plate, is made of a flexible rubber or polymer-based material. The process was introduced in the early 1900s as aniline printing, called this because of the type of inks used. But this name gave way to "flexography" in the late 1940s, the name of the process used exclusively today.

Figure 1-2. Relief image carriers have raised image areas.

LITHOGRAPHY

The lithographic printing principle involves an image carrier with oil-attracting image areas and water-attracting nonimage areas. Because oil and water tend to repel each other, the image and non-image areas on the image carrier are kept distinct from one another. The image carrier used in lithography is referred to as a plate which, when ready to be used for printing, is mounted on a printing press. The lithographic printing press is comprised of a series of rollers and cylinders. One set of rollers brings a water-based solution to the plate and another set brings an oil-based ink (Figure 1-3). The plate is wrapped around a cylinder which in turn contacts the roller systems. The water clings to the nonimage areas of the plate while the oily ink sticks to the image areas of the plate. Then, the inked image is transferred to an intermediate cylinder (called the blanket cylinder). The inked image on the blanket cylinder is forced into contact with the paper by the pressure of the impression cylinder, thus transferring the image. So lithography is really a chemical printing process that is based upon the principle that ink and water repel each other.

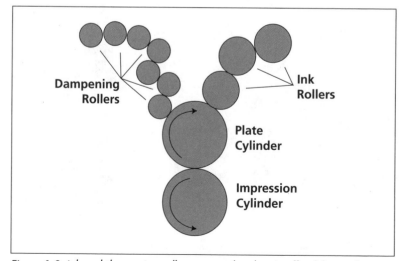

Figure 1-3. Ink and dampening rollers contact the plate in offset lithography.

SCREEN PRINTING

While the screen printing process is used to print only a small portion of the total products that make up the printing market, many
products for which screen printing is used can be printed by no
other method. The principle of the process involves the use of a
stencil that is adhered to a mesh material stretched on a frame
(Figure 1-4). Ink is forced through the mesh and onto a substrate
with pressure exerted by a squeegee. This process is ideally suited
for printing on ridgd materials like metal and glass and is also used
almost exclusively for printing on textiles. The process can also be
used to print on cylindrical surfaces like ceramic mugs and plastic
or glass bottles.

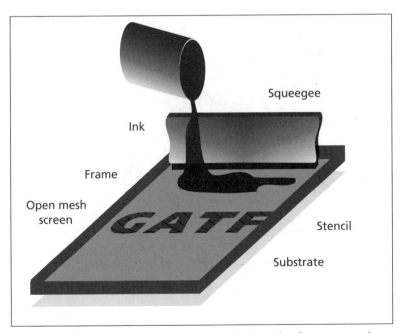

Figure 1-4. The screen printing process pushes ink through a fine screen, with
nonimage areas blocked out by a stencil.

ELECTRONIC METHODS

Over the past several years, many electronic methods of printing have emerged. The oldest of these is the xerographic method, invented by Chester F. Carlson in the late 1930s. The printing process works by producing a positive electric charge on image areas of a selenium drum, while the nonimage areas of the drum have a negative or neutral charge. The drum is rotated over negatively-charged toner particles, which are attracted to the positive charge (image area) of the drum. The toner on the drum is then fused by heat to the paper (Figure 1-5). This printing principle is employed in much of today's low-volume printing equipment, most notably photocopy machines and laser printers. Other major electronic printing methods include ink-jet, thermal wax, and dye sublimation, each of which works on very different principles.

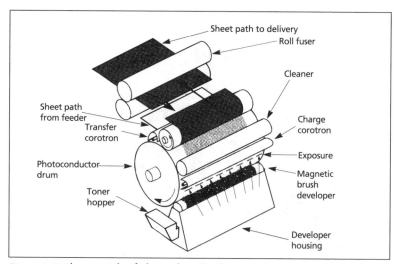

Figure 1-5. The principle of electrophotography.

2 DEFINITION OF GRAVURE PRINTING

Among all the commercial printing processes, gravure is the least known and most often misunderstood. Many graphic arts professionals know that gravure is used to print long-run magazines and catalogs, a variety of packages, and decorated products, but few have ever seen a gravure press in action.

Gravure is an advanced, high-tech process operating the fastest and widest printing presses in the world. It uses a unique image carrier, a gapless cylinder that can be imaged directly from digital data. The image carrier required the development of prepress methods that are radically different from those used by other print processes.

In spite of the huge output of pages, packages, and decorated products, the gravure industry is relatively small in terms of the number of gravure establishments. This concentration of unique technology among a small number of producers has created an industry with its own jargon, trade association, trade magazine, technical education and training programs, and nonprofit educational foundation.

Printers and engravers use the terms gravure, rotogravure, and roto interchangeably. This book is devoted to the webfed rotary process. Sheetfed gravure, fine art intaglio printing, currency printing, and commercial engraving are not included. Unless otherwise stated, the term gravure as used in this book refers to the webfed rotogravure printing process.

Gravure is a mechanically simple printing process. There are four basic components to each printing unit: an engraved cylinder, the ink fountain, the doctor blade, and the impression roller. The

BASIC FACTS AND ADVANTAGES OF THE GRAVURE PROCESS

1. Gravure is an intaglio process. The image to be printed is cut below the surface of the image carrier.

2. Gravure is a direct printing process. The ink is transferred directly to the substrate by the image carrier, giving precise color control throughout the production run.

3. All gravure printing uses fluid inks. They can be formulated to print on any substrate, dry fast, have little show through, and do not rub off the finished product.

4. The image carrier is a gapless cylinder. This produces continuous print and allows for many different image layout options, including random and nested images. The image carrier promotes the optimum use of image space with a minimal amount of unprinted waste.

5. Cylinders are interchangeable. Gravure presses change over quickly, and cylinders can be mounted and prepared for printing off press.

6. All images are screened. Line, process and tints can be combined on the same cylinder. The process is capable of intense color with one pass. The engraved cylinder is capable of laying down a varying ink film thickness where required.

7. Color is controlled by the engraving. Millions of impressions can be produced without color variation.

8. The image carrier is virtually resistant to all chemicals. Inks can be formulated to print on any substrate. They can also be made resistant to products the finished print comes in contact with.

9. Printing is done in-line with inter-station drying. All ink trapping is dry.

10. Gravure is usually a roll-fed or web-fed process. Press operations are efficient and economical with low manning, quick start-ups and re-starts, and low waste. Presses are available in a wide range of widths with the highest continuous operating speeds available in any commercial printing process.

11. Compatible with digital imaging.

simplicity of the process makes it easy to automate and combine with other converting processes such as laminating, sheeting, folding, creasing, diecutting, and slitting. Presses range in size from under 12 in. to as wide as 265 in. (6.7 meters.) Press speeds are limited mostly by substrate and subsequent converting operations. Publication presses routinely run at 3000 feet per minute with packaging presses operating at half that speed, depending on the product being printed.

The gravure press can print on a broad range of substrates from newsprint to sheet vinyl. The image carrier is compatible with the widest range of ink and coating formulations of all the graphic arts printing processes. Solvent- and water-based ink and coatings can be formulated to meet specific product requirements without concern for compatibility with the image carrier.

The image carrier is usually made of a steel or aluminum tube or base electroplated with copper. The image to be reproduced is etched or engraved so that print areas are below the surface of the cylinder. The engraved copper cylinder is then chrome-plated to increase the life of the engraving.

The gravure press is usually built from a basic printing unit (see Figure 2-1). Each unit contains a single cylinder, and prints one color on one side of the web. The printing unit is made up of four essential elements: the gravure cylinder, ink fountain, doctor blade, and impression roller. The gravure cylinder rotates in a tank of fluid ink called the ink fountain. As it rotates, the engraved cells fill with ink, and the entire surface of the cylinder is coated with ink. The excess ink is wiped from the surface of the cylinder by the doctor blade, leaving ink only in the engraved image.

To transfer the ink from the engraved image to the substrate, the impression roll squeezes the moving web of substrate against the engraved gravure cylinder and the ink is drawn out of the engraved cells by capillary action. The web then passes through a hot-air dryer and into the next printing unit.

The number of gravure printing units is determined by the variety of products the printer manufactures. Publication presses are

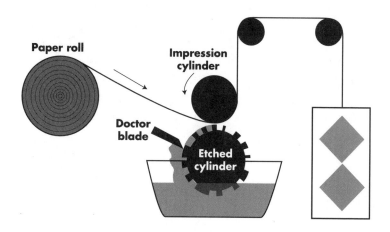

Figure 2-1. Schematic of the basic gravure process.

typically eight units. Packaging and product presses range from one unit to as many as nineteen printing units.

HISTORY OF GRAVURE

Gravure is an intaglio printing process. It refers to a method of printing where the printing plate or image carrier consists of lines or dots cut or engraved below the surface. Intaglio prints are made by covering the image with ink, wiping the excess from the surface, then pressing paper firmly against the plate to transfer ink from the recessed design to the paper.

The first known intaglio plate engraved on metal was used for printing in Germany in 1446 AD. Playing cards were produced by the early engravers, with illustrations consisting of line drawings with close diagonal lines for shading. Artists, working with sharp tools, inscribed copper plates by hand until the invention of chemical etching in the early 1500s.

Chemical etching is a method of fixing an image on a metal surface by the action of a mordant, usually an acid. The surface to be etched is covered with a soft "resist" coating. The artist scraped away the resist layer so that acid could penetrate the resist coating

Figure 2-2. The first gravure engraving, 1446 AD.

and react with the exposed copper during the etching process. Chemical etching also made it possible to use other metals such as zinc, iron, and later steel.

Intaglio plates were not compatible with Gutenberg's letterpress, and it was not possible to combine the two processes. Engravings were produced and tipped in or bound separately as illustrations

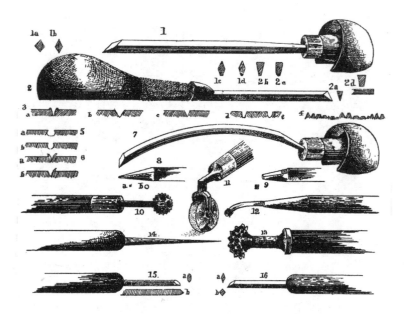

Figure 2-3. Early engraving tools.

for encyclopedias and other reference books. The most famous was the landmark French *Encyclopedie* (1751–1765) which included an entire volume of engravings. Other major applications of engraving included music, maps, stamps, and currency. Engraving remained the dominant method of pictorial reproduction until the latter part of the 19th century.

Letterpress, thanks to foundry type, made literature and the printed word available to mass audiences; intaglio brought illustrations, maps, music, and art to go with it.

The invention of lithography in 1796 presented the first real alternative to intaglio engraving, making it possible to produce a wide range of line and tonal effects that could be created with a crayon rather than engraver's tools.

MODERN GRAVURE

The textile industry pioneered the use of intaglio engraved cylinders to print continuous patterns as early as 1680. In the 1750s textile production was organized into a factory operation. Along with the development of machinery for mass production of textiles came the first patented rotary intaglio printing machine. Thomas Bell received British Patent No. 1443 in 1784. The machine was designed to print on calico cloth. The patent detailed the inking unit, printing cylinder, doctor blade, and impression roll. The printing cylinder was described as having "cores of iron covered with copper or other metal, which can be taken off at pleasure, and by that means fresh patterns put on as often as required."

The invention of photography and the discovery of the halftone screen propelled the next major steps forward for gravure. Development of light-sensitive chemical compounds gave intaglio engravers and printers a new and efficient way to capture images for reproduction. The development of carbon tissue (a light-sensitive gelatin relief resist over a potassium bichromate photosensitive material that could be exposed on paper and transferred) provided a suitable material that could adhere to a copper cylinder and resist the acids used for etching. It took a few years to learn ways to combine these techniques to create the first modern rotogravure cylinders.

The first commercial successes in rotary gravure were due to the efforts of a dynamic entrepreneur named Karel Klic. Klic has been credited with developing the modern gravure process. His major contribution was to expose carbon tissue to a screen, hardening a fine grid, and then exposing the carbon tissue to a continuous-tone positive, causing the cells between the grid lines to harden according to the density of the image. Gravure continued to use continuous-tone positives for engraving until the development of halftone gravure in the 1980s. Gravure continues to be the only printing process that screens all images including solids.

In 1860, Auguste Godchaux, a French publisher who as a young man worked in a textile printing operation, received a patent for a

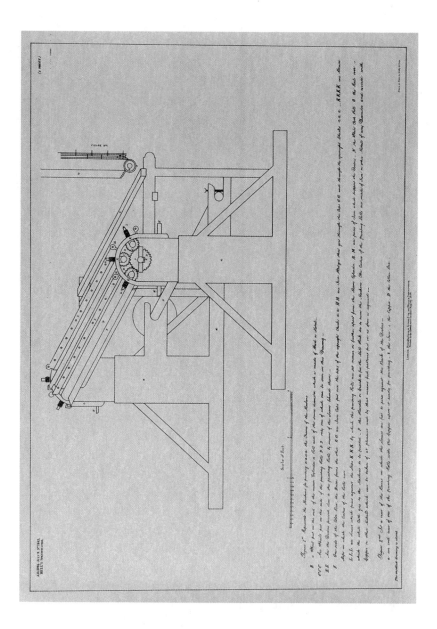

Figure 2-4. The Bell patent.

reel-fed gravure perfector press. The Godchaux firm was very successful and continued to operate until 1940. The 1860 press was in full operation until the firm was liquidated during the German occupation of France during World War II.

Klic's gravure imaging method became widely known at the turn of the century, and the gravure process came to America. The Reich-Wood Company of England built the first gravure presses installed in the United States for the Van Dyke Company of New York in 1903. The first American newspaper to install rotogravure equipment was *The New York Times,* in 1913.

The development of gravure accelerated quickly. Changes and new developments occurred in the engraving methods and in

Figure 2-5. The first New York Times printed by gravure in 1913.

the press equipment. Gravure was introduced into packaging applications. The next logical step was to incorporate other operations such as coating, punching, slitting, cutting and creasing, gluing, and folding with the gravure printing process. By 1933, a single-color gravure press was designed as part of a continuous printing/wrapping operation for Tootsie Rolls. In 1938 the Champlain Company (now the Bobst Group) built two presses for the Jell-O Company. This was the first installation in the United States of large-scale continuous production of multicolor folding cartons with printing and diecutting in line. This new concept won the All-American Packaging Competition Award in 1939. Champlain also pioneered the development of electronic register controls. The first set of electronic controls to operate from a single register mark was developed in 1937.

Figure 2-6. Early gravure press line.

In the 1960s, electromechanical engraving machines were introduced to the U.S. market. The first electronically controlled engraving machines were developed by the Hell Corporation (now Heidelberg Prepress). The machine uses either an electronic scanning system or digital input to drive a diamond cutting tool, engraving mechanically rather than by chemical etching.

Figure 2-7. The first electronically controlled engraving machine, made by the Hell Corporation.

THE ROOTS OF GRAVURE

3000 BC	Relief printing on clay from stone cylinder (Sumeria)
100–200 AD	Reproduction from wood blocks by rubbings (China)
600-700	Wood block printing on textiles (Egypt)
764	First wood block prints (Japan)
1151	First European paper (Spain)
1402	Playing cards produced from wood blocks (Germany)
1436	First use of relief, royal seals and signatures (England, Henry VI)
c. 1439	Gutenberg develops the printing press using movable type
1446	First intaglio plate engraved in metal used for printing
1455	Completion of Gutenberg Bible (Germany)
1505	Chemical etching
1784	First rotary gravure press patented by Thomas Bell (England)
1796	Invention of lithography (Alois Senefelder)
1806	First steel plates used for intaglio engraving
1814	First commercial letterpress with impression cylinder (England)
1816–1838	Invention and development of photography (France)
1844	First letterpress with an image carrier cylinder (Richard Hoe, United States)
1852	Invention of photo resists
1860	Invention of halftone screen
1864	Invention of carbon tissue
1865	First roll-fed letterpress with image carrier and impression cylinders (United States)
1868	First rotary litho press with impression cylinders and zinc plates on image carrier cylinders
c.1870	First automatic in-line folders (United States)
1890	Development of photoengraving (Fawcett)
1891	First commercial manufacturing of carbon tissue paper for etching (Autotype Co., England)
1913	First gravure newspaper magazine (New York Times)
1920–1930	Ballard shell, Dultgen engraving introduced
1937	Electronic register controls
1966	Electrostatic assist (United States)
1968	Electromechanical cylinder engraving (Germany)
1983	Digital electronic engraving

3 GRAVURE PRODUCTS AND MARKETS

The gravure market is divided into three distinct segments: publication, packaging, and product or specialty gravure. Each market segment has its own distinct subcategories.

PUBLICATION GRAVURE

The publication gravure industry is made up of a small number of very large companies operating presses that range in size from 72 to 125 in. wide. This market segment produces magazines, Sunday supplements, newspaper inserts, catalogs, and miscellaneous commercial printing (flyers, direct mail, forms, brochures, etc.) Seventy-two percent of the standard magazine pages, 63% of the digest pages, and 100% of the tabloid pages are printed gravure. Total copy count has averaged about 2.75 billion over the past five years.

Figure 3-1. Many consumer magazines are printed by gravure.

Gravure remains the process of choice for long-run, high-quality publication printing accounting for about thirty magazine titles. Gravure is used by all of the top ten publications. Sunday magazines or "roto sections" are about 90% gravure, and newspaper inserts are estimated at 12%. Nationally distributed titles such as *Parade Magazine* and *USA Weekend* dominate this market segment.

Figure 3-2. Catalog publishing depends on quality color reproduction. This is gravure's fastest growing market segment.

Catalogs are defined as sixteen or more bound pages designed specifically to market products and/or services of an organization. This is the fastest growing segment in gravure publications with the current market share at 35% and growing.

In the publication segment, gravure is used to print advertising flyers, direct mail pieces, brochures, and magazine inserts. Miscellaneous commercial gravure printing includes annual reports and books, financial and bank printing, playing cards, and chart paper.

PACKAGING GRAVURE

Packaging is a part of everyday life. This industry is made up of a very diverse array of companies accounting for about 6% of all manufactured products. Gravure-printed packaging has three major subcategories: folding cartons, labels and wrappers, and flexible packaging.

Folding cartons are printed primarily by gravure and offset lithography with flexography just entering the market. Some examples include soap and detergent cartons, tobacco cartons, food packaging, automotive parts packaging, and point-of-purchase displays. Approximately 30% of this market is gravure.

Gravure-printed labels and wrappers include roll and sheet labels that are applied to cans, unprinted cartons, composite cans, bottles, and other containers. Labels and wrappers are printed on coated-one-side (C1S) paper, paper/foil laminates, metallized paper, and film. Gravure printing accounts for about 20% of the label market.

Flexible packaging is made up of converted materials intended to hold or contain products weighing less than 25 lb. Flexible packaging operations include the manufacture of a wide variety of products in non-rigid packages made of paper, plastic film, foil laminates, and combinations of these substrates. It is covered under nine different standard industrial classification (SIC) codes. Gravure is used in about 30% of this market. The versatility of the gravure press makes the combination of converting and printing in line very cost effective. Coating, laminating, cutting, creasing, slitting, and diecutting are a few of the converting operations commonly combined with gravure printing.

PRODUCT GRAVURE

Product gravure makes up a very diverse product group. In many cases the manufacturers do not consider themselves printers and

Figure 3-3. Folding cartons and flexible packaging are major parts of gravure's market segment.

consider gravure applications as part of the manufacturing process. This segment includes gift wrap, wallcoverings, decorative laminates, vinyl floor coverings, postage stamps, and a large variety of vinyl and plastic products. These diverse products include:

- Shower curtains
- Place mats
- Tablecloths
- Unsupported wall and counter coverings
- Ceiling tiles
- Automobile upholstery
- Automobile trim, including side and door panels
- Vinyl fabric for outdoor furniture such as umbrellas and chairs
- Infants' products such as highchairs, strollers, and bibs
- Vinyl fabrics for luggage and other decorative vinyl

Other unclassified gravure printed products include a variety of specialty products that use gravure for decorating and coating, often in-line with other manufacturing processes. (The total market

Figure 3-4. Wood grain, solid laminate patterns, and product trademarking are often printed by gravure.

value for the product gravure market segment has not been calculated.) These products include:

- Cigarette filter tips
- Heat transfer paper
- Marbled book endpapers
- Coated cover papers
- Decalcomania
- Bottle and heat-seal closures
- Hot stamp foils
- Pill and candy trademarking
- Windshield tinting
- House siding and paneling

PREPRESS SERVICE HOUSES

Service houses provide a variety of prepress and engraving services to both gravure printers and their customers. All gravure publication printers provide prepress services in house as well as plating and engraving. In comparison, a relatively few packaging and product gravure plants have their own cylinder engraving operations resulting in the majority of gravure cylinders being purchased from service houses. Digital prepress services are growing at a rapid rate and are being provided by customers, service houses, and printers.

4 THE GRAVURE IMAGE CARRIER

The gravure image carrier is a cylinder that is either engraved or etched with the pattern or image that is to be printed. This chapter will discuss the underlying structure that supports the engraved image, how it is manufactured, the materials that are used, and the critical specifications necessary for it to run on the gravure press.

CYLINDER BASES

The cylinder base is the physical structure that supports the engraved image used to transfer ink to the substrate on a gravure press. There are basically two different types of cylinder bases—the

Figure 4-1. A variety of different-sized gravure cylinders.

mandrel or sleeve and the integral shaft. A third type of cylinder is called a Ballard shell.

The sleeve must be mounted on a shaft that fits exactly into the sleeve and is designed to mount on the press. Sleeve cylinders are smaller and lighter in weight than shaft cylinders and have a lower initial cost. They are less expensive to store and transport. On the down side, different shafts are used in printing, prepping, and engraving and can be the source of inaccuracy. Sleeves are used very successfully on narrow web presses printing lightweight material.

Integral shaft cylinders have permanently attached shafts. Each shaft is made with a gudgeon that is shrunk and welded onto each end of the cylinder. The shaft is precisely machined and fitted with a bearing inner race. The dimensions of the bearing inner race are critical because it is the bearing surface for the cylinder when it is mounted in the press. Integral shaft cylinders, when they are well maintained, provide a very accurate support structure for the gravure engraving.

The Ballard shell is made through plating technology rather than base design. It can be applied to both sleeve and integral shaft cylinders. Basically the Ballard shell is a cylinder with a base of copper coated with a "separation layer." The cylinder is then copper plated again before engraving. The cylinder is then finished as described below. The advantage of using Ballard shell technology is that the engraved image can be manually stripped off the cylinder without having to dechrome and grind the cylinder

Figure 4-2. Ballard shell stripping.

before replating. This technology has been used almost exclusively by publication gravure printers.

BASE MATERIALS

The majority of cylinder bases are made of steel. Hot-finished and cold-drawn steel tubing are excellent base materials and are used most often. They have relatively close tolerances, good surface finish, and are generally free of material defects. Steel has minimal deflection tendencies, requires only a moderate amount of machining and balancing, and is easily plated. Steel tubing is available either hot-finished or cold-drawn with a choice of wall thicknesses. Large, high-performance cylinders for publication printing are all cold-drawn steel.

Aluminum cylinder bases are used less frequently for packaging and product printing. Most aluminum bases are sleeve types. Lightweight nickel sleeves and synthetic sleeves are also used on a limited basis. The lighter weight reduces shipping costs and makes cylinder handling in the pressroom very easy. These lighter materials are limited to applications that are not subject to deflection during press operations. Regardless of the base material selected, the surface must be prepared to accept copper plating.

BASE SPECIFICATIONS

Each gravure press comes with a set of drawings for the precise manufacture of the cylinder base that will fit that particular press. Cylinder bases are essentially machine parts and are not necessarily compatible with other machines. The tubes, shafts, and inner races requires precise machining to meet the mechanical requirements of a gravure press.

BALANCING

The high speeds of a gravure press require that the gravure printing cylinder be balanced. Just as out-of-balance tires on a car cause vibration, an unbalanced cylinder will cause excessive vibrations on the press that will limit printing speeds and cause numerous mechanical problems, resulting in print defects.

Imbalance occurs when the mass center of a rotating object does not coincide with the rotational axis as determined by its supporting bearings. A cylinder which is not restrained by bearings will revolve about its mass center. When restrained by bearings, it is forced to rotate about an axis other than its mass center, introducing centrifugal forces that cause vibrations. Balancing is the operation that eliminates the vibrations by redistributing the mass of the cylinder so its center of gravity lies in the same axis as the supporting bearings. All new cylinder bases require balancing as one of the final manufacturing steps.

Two types of balance are addressed. Static balance involves only gravity and is obtained when the cylinder base is at rest. This type of balancing does not meet the needs of a high-speed gravure press. Today gravure cylinders are dynamically balanced, correcting imbalance that can occur as a result of centrifugal forces at high press speeds.

SURFACE MATERIALS

Copper and chrome are deposited on the surface of the gravure cylinder base by the process of electroplating. The plating process is a complicated electrochemical process, similar to that used in a number of other industrial processes.

Photopolymers, ceramic coatings, and plastics have been developed and tested as substitutes

Figure 4-3. Full-immersion tank.

for copper and chrome. Most of these developments remain proprietary processes and are not generally commercially available.

COPPER

The copper-plated surface of a gravure cylinder has three functions: engravability, stability in the press, and reproducibility. Copper is

Figure 4-4. A stone polishing machine.

suitable for both chemical and electromechanical engraving. It etches or engraves easily with very predictable results. Copper is strong enough to ensure that the engraved image remains stable under high nip pressure in the press. It also fulfills the final requirement of reproducibility. Copper can be removed, replaced, cut, and polished with predictable results.

Copper polishing. Copper polishing is the preparation of the copper surface with the help of abrasives. Copper is polished at different stages during the cylinder making process. Usually copper is polished after the copper surface has been machined for size either on a lathe or with a machine tool. After proofing and corrections, the copper is polished to have a uniform surface for chrome plating. Polishing after electromechanical engraving removes any burrs that may have been left by the diamond engraving head.

Polishing stones or wheels, polishing paper, lapping film, polishing pastes, and buffing wheels are all employed to achieve the required surface finish. Polishing is done by hand as well as on machines designed specifically for this purpose.

CHROME

Chrome plating over the copper surface extends the printing life of the engraved cylinder. The chrome gives the copper surface protection against abrasive wear caused by friction. Like copper plating, chrome plating is reproducible with predictable results.

Chrome polishing. Chrome polishing is the final step of cylinder preparation. The cylinder must be finished to minimize wear on long or repeated pressruns. Cylinder polishing is confined to the surface of the cylinder. Polishing is accomplished both by hand or in a polishing machine. Newer developments in chrome plating chemistry have minimized the amount of polishing necessary to produce a good cylinder.

Polishing cannot correct mistakes made in preceding process steps. The chrome layer follows the surface profile of the copper layer. If the copper surface is too smooth or too rough, chrome polishing cannot make up for the defect.

5 GRAVURE CYLINDER ENGRAVING

Gravure is unique in that it is the only commercial printing process that has the ability to control both the area of the coverage and the thickness of the ink film. This is achieved by engraving recessed cells of varying area and depth in the surface of the image carrier. We are in the midst of a technical revolution in which engraving technology is rapidly evolving.

CARBON TISSUE

The earliest recognized process of using carbon tissue is described here for historical reference. It is rarely used today except as a fine art form. Carbon tissue or pigment paper is made by coating a mixture of gelatin (emulsion) and pigment on paper and then drying. The carbon tissue is exposed under a rotogravure screen and an assembly of continuous-tone positives. The screen exposure provides lines of hardened gelatin, while the positive exposure results in differential hardening of the gelatin to varying depths depending on the density of the tones in the positive. The carbon tissue is then transferred to the copper-plated cylinder. The backing paper is removed and the soluble gelatin (that was not exposed) is washed away with hot water. A print is left on the copper cylinder where the tone image is represented by areas of gelatin of different thicknesses overlaid with a pattern of screen lines of thick gelatin. Before etching, the cylinder is staged—meaning all parts of the cylinder that are not to be etched and are not protected by resist must be painted over with a waterproof paint or varnish. An etching solution of ferric chloride is used to etch or dissolve the copper through the gelatin resist. The differential etching is controlled by the amount of resist,

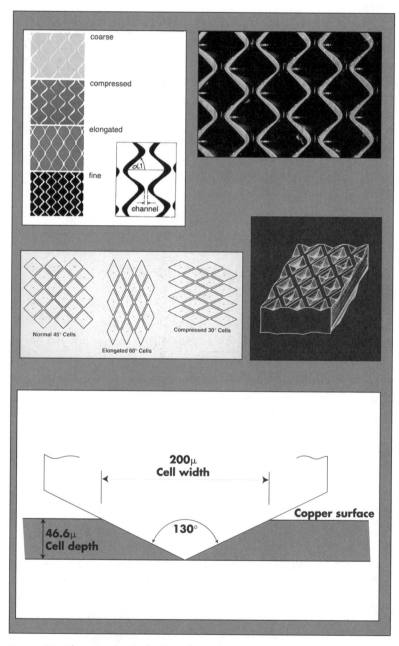

Figure 5-1. Electromechanical cell configurations.

strength of the etching solution, time, temperature, and the skill and craftsmanship of the etcher. This method often required numerous hand corrections to achieve the desired results.

DIRECT TRANSFER

Beginning in the late 1950s a number of products were developed that were easier to handle than carbon tissue, but were still designed for chemical engraving. Chemical engravings today are prepared by using what is called a stencil resist which applies photo-sensitive material directly to the cylinder. They are called "stencil" resists because the resultant developed image areas after exposure to the film are bare copper. There are a number of techniques in use to achieve this result.

ELECTROMECHANICAL ENGRAVING

Electromechanical engraving appeared as a commercial process in the late 1960s and has almost completely replaced earlier chemical processes. In its simplest form, the engraving machine has three basic parts: a scanning head and cylindrical drum for mounting copy, or a digital input device; a control panel and power supply; and an engraving head and cylinder mounting station.

SUMMARY OF CURRENT TECHNOLOGY

The gravure engraving process today includes chemical engraving, usually employing a method called direct transfer, electromechanical engraving, and recently-introduced laser technology.

ELECTROMECHANICAL ENGRAVING

Electromechanical engraving freed gravure image processing from carbon tissue transfers and chemical etching. This method of cylinder preparation uses a diamond stylus that vibrates at more than 4500 times per second, cutting a diamond-shaped cell in the copper-plated cylinder. The input information that drives the diamond stylus is generated by a scanner or by a digital file.

The physical volume of the electromechanical cell is approximately 30% less than the chemically-engraved cell, but other factors play a part in overcoming this difference. The inverted diamond shape of the cell provides a superior ink release compensating for the reduced cell volume.

In the solid areas of the image, the diamond stylus can be programmed to cut a channel between the cells. The channel enhances the flow of ink from the cells and produces a smoother coverage in the solid areas.

DIRECT DIGITAL ENGRAVING

Direct digital engraving refers to the filmless transfer of the image from a digital file to the image carrier via an electromechanical engraver. In a filmless environment, all image corrections are done in the digital file, eliminating the need to correct film and/or cylinders. This significantly reduces the time required for the manufacturing cycle and produces consistent quality. A duplicate cylinder can be made from the digital data, thus minimizing the variables inherent in the use of film. This process can be repeated as often as

Figure 5-2. Daetwyler LaserStar engraver.

required. This is a great advantage for packaging and product gravure printers who often repeat the printing of a design for years.

LASER ENGRAVING

Recently introduced laser engraving technology is being Beta-site tested at the time of this writing. Although laser and electron-beam technologies were researched in the 1970s, they were always deemed too expensive for commercial use. The newest entry into the engraving market has developed a new alloy that can be plated and machined using existing equipment currently handling copper. The laser engraver is designed to be six times faster than existing electromechanical equipment. The equipment is also designed to integrate efficiently into existing production environments capable of sharing the same prepress technology. We expect that commercial results and the adoption of laser technology will be completed in the next couple of years.

ELECTRON-BEAM ENGRAVING

The Hell company developed electron-beam engraving techniques in Germany in the late 1980s. This technology, working in a vacuum, could engrave cells at speeds reportedly up to 150,000 cells per second in a copper image carrier using digital imaging information as input. After early field testing, the equipment was withdrawn from the market because it was too expensive to be competitive in the commercial market. An interest remains in electron-beam technology. As other technologies advance, it may again become a viable option for gravure engraving.

CYLINDER PROOFING

Proofing of the engraved gravure cylinder is a critical part of the prepress process. All cylinders engraved by chemical etching or electromechanical engraving using analog scanning are proofed either on a multiunit proof press for publication cylinders or on a single-color proof press for packaging and product cylinders. The proofing process is performed on the actual substrate to be

Figure 5-3. Single-unit gravure packaging proof press.

printed, with inks that are comparable to the final pressrun, except they are slower drying to facilitate cleanup. As more and more engravings are generated from digital information, the need for press proofing is being reduced.

Proofs printed by digital printers directly from the digital data are increasingly common in all three gravure market segments.

HALFTONE GRAVURE

The Gravure Association of America published Publication Half-tone Specifications for Gravure in 1988. They have been updated periodically to reflect advancements in gravure prepress technology. One of the most significant advances in gravure technology was the successful use of digital input in the form of halftones, to drive electromechanical engraving machines. This eliminated gravure's dependence on continuous-tone film. These specifications made it possible to use the same film for both gravure and offset.

6 GRAVURE PRESSES

T he limited number of press components and simplicity of design makes gravure easy to automate, simple to operate, and very adaptable to inline converting operations. The simplicity also ensures consistently high print quality even in extremely long print runs.

Depending on the product to be produced, presses can be 4–240 in. wide. Since one color is printed at a time, the number of press units in the press depends on the printer's needs. Single-color units are used for a variety of ink, coating, and adhesive applications. Most publication presses are eight colors. Specialty products such as lottery tickets may have as many as eighteen individual units.

All gravure presses are custom built, designed to satisfy the customer's specifications based on the end product to be produced. For example a packaging press for producing labels may be 26 in. wide with seven print units; a press for producing vinyl floor covering may be 12 feet wide with six print units; both presses are identical in principle, but customized for the end product.

To determine the features of a gravure press, the following factors must be determined:

- Caliper of the substrates to be printed
- Minimum and maximum web widths to be printed
- Minimum and maximum cylinder circumference (this determines page size or print repeats)
- Press speed as determined by in-line converting operations
- Tension ranges based on the physical characteristics of the substrates to be printed
- Number of print units

- Dryers, sized and zoned to handle press speed, substrate, and the type of inks and coatings to be applied
- Infeed unit determined by the specific needs of the substrates to be handled
- Outfeed unit determined by the substrate and the in-line converting operations following the last print unit
- Drives, the power source determined by substrate, press speed, and tension ranges
- Controls, determined by the amount of automation desired (these include on-line video monitoring, register controls, preset job setup, production statistics, waste analysis, electrostatic assist, automated ink dispensing and viscosity control, and a long list of other on-line controls to assist in pressroom management.)

SECTIONS OF THE PRESS

SUBSTRATE SUPPLY

The substrate supply section includes the reel stand, splicing unit, web guide, pre-treatment, and infeed tension control. All web-fed gravure presses start from a reel stand that unwinds the roll of substrate to be printed. The infeed is critical for web and tension control throughout the rest of the press. High-speed presses have what is called a two-position reel stand. This allows two rolls of substrate to be mounted on the press at one time. For presses printing light weight materials, the unwind unit is equipped to splice a new roll to the end of the expiring roll. This allows continuous operation of the press when the rolls are spliced together. Presses printing heavyweight material such as sheet vinyl or thick board have a web accumulator or festoon that is described in detail later in this chapter.

GRAVURE PRINTING UNIT

At the heart of the gravure press is the printing unit. It contains the following five basic components regardless of the application:

- The engraved cylinder (image carrier)

Figure 6-1. A large gravure press used to print packaging and wall coverings. (Courtesy Bobst Champlain)

- An ink fountain, a large pan positioned beneath the cylinder that extends the width of the printing unit
- A doctor blade assembly consisting of a doctor blade, doctor blade holder, and oscillation mechanism
- An impression system to hold the substrate against the engraved cylinder to facilitate ink transfer
- A dryer that provides heated air to dry the moving web before it enters the next printing unit

DELIVERY SECTION

The delivery section always follows the last printing unit. Publication presses are equipped with upper and lower folders to convert the full web into slit ribbons that are gathered and folded into signatures. Packaging and product presses have a wide variety of inline converting operations available depending on the product being printed. Cutters, creasers, and diecutters are just a few of the options available.

PRESS CONFIGURATIONS FOR PUBLICATION

Gravure publication presses are designed for high speed and high color quality. Publication products include magazines, catalogs, newspaper inserts, Sunday newspaper magazines, and advertising printing. Typically a publication gravure press offers:

- High-speed production (3000+ feet per minute)
- Variable cutoffs
- Inline finishing (multiple printed ribbons must be folded and assembled into complete publications on the press, or delivered as folded signatures to the bindery)
- Adaptability to a wide variety of substrates including lightweight, lower-cost papers
- Low start-up and running waste
- Color consistency throughout the pressrun

The majority of U.S. publication gravure presses have eight or ten printing units that print four or five colors on each side of the web. Web widths on newer presses range from 72 to 143 in. Typically a press can produce up to six different products, with pagination of the signature from 8 to 144 pages. In-line converting operations include:

- Folding
- Stitching
- Auto stacking
- Inserting cards and coupons
- Gluing
- Perforating
- Imprinting
- Coating
- Trimming

GRAVURE FOLDERS

A gravure publication press can be equipped with a variety of folders. The purpose of the folder is to take single or multiple webs from the printing units, slit them into ribbons, assemble the ribbons in aligned groups, and pass them through a cut-and-fold mechanism to produce a folded signature. Folding technology can only be described with a set of unique terms. Understanding this terminology is essential for anyone buying print, planning layouts, engraving cylinders, or operating a publication gravure press.

FOLDER TERMINOLOGY

Ribbons are formed by slitting the web as it emerges from the last print unit. These ribbons continue into folders where they are folded and recombined in various ways.

Angle bars change the orientation of the ribbon by turning it at a 90° angle. Singly or in succession, angle bars are used to reorient a web for reverse-direction processing, additional folding, or to superimpose a group of ribbons to obtain desired pagination.

Cylinder imposition is the way pages are laid out on the publication cylinder. The pages must match the configuration of the folder in order for every signature to have pages in the correct sequence and orientation in the finished product. A variety of cylinder layouts can be used depending on the type of folder, page size, page count, width of the press, and the final trimmed page size. A one-up imposition refers to a cylinder layout with one set of unique pages. A two-up cylinder repeats the page layout twice around the circumference of the cylinder and so on up to six- or eight-around on the newest presses.

TYPES OF FOLDERS

Variable cutoff folders are the most commonly used folders with publication gravure presses. They enable gravure printers to supply print buyers with a wide variety of product sizes.

- Upper and lower folders make up the two folder sections of a gravure press. The upper folder typically slits the web into ribbons, then uses angle bars to superimpose or gather the ribbons.
- The lower folder cuts and folds the gathered ribbons into signatures. The final size of the signature can be any desired length and width based on the dimensions of the printing cylinder.
- Former folders fold a moving web or ribbon in the grain direction of the paper (parallel to the web path). They are also referred to as long-grain folders.
- Combination folders are capable of a wide variety of folds in both the grain direction and cross-grain direction. Typically the first fold is accomplished over a V-shaped former board and the second fold is at a right angle. Additional folds may be completed before the ribbon leaves the folder.
- Gravure lower folders are often variable in size. They are capable of producing products with different cutoffs, from different cylinder diameters, and can accommodate four-, six-, or eight-page layouts around the cylinder.
- Ribbon jaw folders assemble the ribbons then cut and fold them in the cross-grain direction. The folding action is accom-

plished by the jaw assembly and can be either a single or double
parallel fold.

- Chopper folders have formers and are used to produce two-on
  signatures or single signatures by alternating the deliveries. The
  fold is accomplished over the former in the grain direction.

PRESS CONFIGURATIONS FOR PACKAGING

Gravure presses designed to produce packaging are divided into
two distinct groups by substrate. Lightweight substrates are used to
produce, but are not limited to, flexible packaging, paper and foil
labels, and wraps. Typical products produced with heavyweight substrates include folding cartons, soap cartons, and beverage containers. The ranges of weights overlap in the mid-range making it possible to print a variety of products and substrates on the same press.
The single most important difference between the two different
classes of press is the register and tension control systems.

Packaging presses usually are combined with at least one in-line
converting operation. Some common in-line operations include:

- Coating
- Creasing
- Diecutting
- Embossing
- Laminating
- Sheeting
- Slitting
- Punching/perforating
- Rewinding

Gravure presses designed to print lightweight materials such as
extensible films, paper, and paper/film/foil laminations usually
have at least eight print units. Web widths are typically 18–60 in.
Flexible packaging presses also have options for reverse printing
units, preconditioning systems to heat the substrate before printing,
and cooling units or chill rollers to cool temperature-sensitive films

and laminations. Corona treaters can also be added before printing to insure good ink and coating adhesion.

Presses designed to handle heavy substrates must have reel stands designed to handle the weight of the substrates. Presses in this group are typically built between 44–216 in. wide. They run at slower speeds than presses running lightweight substrates. A folding carton press with an in-line cutter/creaser will generally run at 600–800 feet per minute.

SPLICING

Splicing is the attachment of a new roll of substrate to the end of an expiring roll. If the press is equipped with a rewind unit for the printed web, it will also be equipped with a splicing unit. Because of the variety of substrates, there are varieties of splicing options available. There are two basic types of splices: the lap splice and the butt splice. For flexible materials of low caliper (i.e., films, foil, laminations, and papers), a lap splice is recommended.

A lap splice involves joining a new roll to the expiring roll by gluing, done at the operating speed of the press. It is often referred to as a flying splice, meaning that rolls are joined "on the fly." Maintaining good tension and register control as the splice moves through the printing units is necessary to avoid unnecessary waste.

A butt splice involves joining two webs with tape. They are butted end to end rather than overlapping because of the thickness of the substrate. To make a butt splice while the press is running, the press is equipped with a festoon.

The festoon is a series of rolls following the unwind section of the press that gradually collapse to continue feeding substrate through the press when the unwind is momentarily stopped to execute a butt splice. When the splice is completed, the festoon rolls gradually return to their original position, ready for the next splice.

7 INK TRANSFER AND DRYING

The ink fountain is one of the five basic components of the gravure printing unit. It is a tank or pan positioned beneath the printing cylinder that spans the width of the press. The engraved cylinder revolves partially submerged in a bath of fluid ink.

Presses that are designed to run a broad range of cylinder circumferences have an inner pan fitted in the ink fountain. The vertically adjustable pan helps keep the cylinder submerged in ink, and reduces unnecessary turbulence in the fluid ink.

The impression roll rides on top of the engraved cylinder, revolving in the opposite direction. When pressure is applied to the impression roll, it squeezes the substrate against the engraved cylinder. The point of contact between the engraved cylinder and the impression roll is call the "nip."

At the nip, the ink must come in contact with the substrate in order for ink to transfer from the engraved cells to the substrate.

Dwell time is the period of time the substrate is in physical contact with the engraved cylinder. This is the time available for the ink to transfer from the cylinder to the substrate. If the width of the nip and web speed is known, the dwell time can be calculated. For instance, a press running at 2,000 feet per minute with a 9-in. diameter impression roll and ⅛-in. nip has a dwell time of about 0.00125 seconds. If the contact does not occur during this brief period because of irregularities in the substrate or a variety of other reasons, complete ink transfer cannot take place. The resulting defect is referred to as "missing dots," "skipped dots," or "snowflaking." This defect can be remedied on a gravure press with the applica-

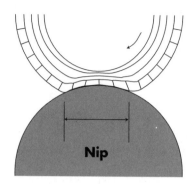

Figure 7-1. Schematic cross section at the gravure nip.

tion of electrostatic assist. This will be discussed in greater detail later in chapter 9.

On some presses an ink fountain roller is used to apply ink to the engraved cylinder. It is positioned underneath the cylinder and helps to fill all the engraved cells with ink to assist in reducing "missing dots." This is especially important on very high-speed presses where there is a very brief dwell time, and on very wide presses where ink circulation can be a problem.

VISCOSITY

Viscosity is the most important characteristic of gravure ink that can be controlled by the press operator. It is measured to monitor and maintain desirable ink flow characteristics. Simply defined, viscosity is a measure of a fluid's ability to flow. Gravure printing requires ink viscosity that will ensure uniform print quality and color consistency throughout the print run. Viscosity influences drying speed, printability, trapping, printed gloss, ink adhesion, and ink holdout.

Ink temperature has a very complex effect on ink performance. Solvent-based as well as water-based inks are sensitive to temperature changes. As ink temperature increases, viscosity drops rapidly, requiring less solvent to maintain desired printing viscosity. If the ink is overcooled it will increase in viscosity, requiring more solvent to reduce viscosity. This can cause another set of printing problems. Viscosity control is imperative to produce good print quality.

MEASURING VISCOSITY

The easiest method to measure viscosity is the efflux cup. It is a small cup with a hole in the bottom and a handle at the top. The length of time in seconds that it takes a full cup of ink to empty through the hole (orifice) is the viscosity measurement reported in seconds for a specific cup number. The thinner the ink, the faster it drains from the cup. The most common efflux cups are the Shell cup, Zahn cup, ISO cup, and Hiccup. They differ in size and shape as well as construction.

The procedure for measuring viscosity starts by submerging the cup below the surface of the ink. Raise the filled cup in a smooth continuous motion. Start a stopwatch the instant the cup breaks the surface, and stop the watch when the continuous ink flow from the hole stops. The viscosity is recorded in seconds for a specific cup number. It is desirable to average three separate readings, which should be within 0.5 seconds of each other. Since ink temperature affects viscosity, it is advisable to note the temperature when viscosity readings are taken.

Automated viscosity controls have various levels of sophistication. They measure and control viscosity continually rather than on a periodic basis. They all work on a similar principle; a sensor is immersed in the ink and measures viscosity by sensing the drag on the sensor, which is driven at a constant speed.

The method of maintaining constant viscosity is either by adding fresh ink to the fountain

Figure 7-2. Measuring the viscosity of ink.

or by adding solvent to compensate for solvent evaporation. Solvent addition must be done with care to avoid spoiling the ink or negatively affecting print quality.

DRYING

Drying speed is affected by the evaporation rate of the solvents used to adjust viscosity. Ideally, the ink manufacturer will recommend a solvent blend that is compatible with the ink formulation and the evaporative rate necessary to dry the ink at production speeds.

DRYER FUNCTION

Dryers are necessary for high-speed gravure printing because the web cannot run straight through multiple printing stations without making contact with other rollers. The ink must be dry enough not to stick to any rolls it contacts with the printed side of the web. Dryers would not be necessary if the press ran slow enough for the ink to air-dry.

The basic principles of drying are called the "three Ts": time, temperature, and turbulence. Time is the most important. All liquids will dry when they are given enough time. The time that is required to dry the ink in relation to the web speed for the desired production determines the dryer length.

Temperature is an easy factor to control. Heat sources for gravure dryers include steam, gas, electric, thermic oil, gas/oil combination, and waste heat from an incinerator. The addition of heat quickly increases drying speed. Too much heat can cause the substrate to shrink, stretch, curl, or become brittle. Excess heat can also cause many ink and coating defects. If the ink film dries too fast, it can skin over (that is, dry on the surface), trapping moisture underneath. This condition can result in retained odors, as well as ink picking on subsequent rolls and blocking when the printed product is rewound or stacked.

Turbulence is the movement of air. Turbulence involves nozzle design, velocity, and air volume. The air turbulence at the web surface is very important. In the dryer, the speed or velocity of air movement and its direction can greatly affect drying speed. Uniform distribution of the air supply across the web is necessary for consistent drying.

Gravure dryers are designed based on the substrate, ink, and coating, specified by the printer. They must be easily accessible for cleaning and constructed to strict safety standards if the press is printing with volatile solvents. The solvent load must be the heaviest possible load for each print unit. Solvent load is the maximum gallons per minute of solvents to be evaporated. The press manufacturer estimates this number and designs the exhaust size so that it cannot be reduced below this level. The estimated solvent load is based on press width, press speed, square inches covered per pound of ink, average percent of printed coverage, percent solvents in the ink, and weight of a gallon of typical solvent. Most dryers that handle volatile vapors are equipped with an LEL (lower explosive limit) detector or control. It measures the concentration of solvent vapors in air as a percent of the level that will explode if exposed to a spark or flame. If the solvent concentration exceeds a safe level for operating, the press will be stopped automatically. The real value to using this system comes from reducing the exhaust volume on print units that are applying a small amount of ink, saving a considerable amount of energy.

Dryers are constructed so that airflow can be controlled in specific sections or "zones" of the drying unit. In a single-zone dryer, the temperature and airflow are the same throughout the unit. Multi-zone units can operate independently with individual temperature controls for the different zones and air recirculation from one zone to another within the unit. Multi-zone dryers are ideal for water-based inks, adhesives, and a variety of coatings.

A dryer is considered in neutral balance when the amount of air exhausted is equal to the amount of supply air necessary to meet the production requirements of the press. This condition is difficult to achieve and maintain. When the dryer draws a small amount of room air into the dryer along with the web, this creates a slight negative imbalance, which is an ideal operating condition. Positive balance occurs when dryer air spills into the pressroom, raising the level of solvent fumes and creating a generally unhealthy and uncomfortable condition.

WATER-BASED INK

Water-based inks contain little or no volatile solvent and do not constitute an explosive hazard. However, as relative humidity increases, water evaporates more slowly. To keep the humidity from increasing in a dryer, it is necessary to increase the amount of exhaust air. Increasing the turbulence where the air impinges on the printed web is more effective than increasing the temperature when drying water-based inks and coating. Excessive heat can cause extensible substrates to stretch and paper-based substrates to shrink, leading to register and tension control problems.

Press speed determines the amount of time the web is in the dryer. For high-speed printing with water-based inks, dryers are built with longer web paths to insure enough time to dry the ink.

ENVIRONMENTAL COMPLIANCE

The solvents used in most gravure ink formulations are designated as volatile organic compounds (VOC). When exposed to sunlight, VOCs contribute to the formation of smog and are therefore listed as hazardous air pollutants (HAP) by the Environmental Protection Agency. Regulations established on May 15, 1995 require that all presses emitting over 100 tons per year of solvent vapors have pollution control devices. The printer's options for pollution control includes low-VOC or water-based ink, solvent recovery, and fume incineration.

WATER-BASED INK
Water-based ink technology has been around since the 1960s. It is the least costly compliance option, but today's technology has many limitations. Water systems require as much as five times the amount

of energy that is required to dry solvent inks. Water inks have been successful in packaging and product applications where press speeds have a tendency to be slower than publication gravure press speeds. Acceptable print quality has been achieved on coated board, vinyl, aluminum foil, and lightweight papers.

SOLVENT RECOVERY

A solvent recovery system removes solvent fumes from the dryer exhaust air and collects the solvent for reuse. Solvent recovery systems are excellent for multiple press operations where the solvents can be selected for easy recovery and reuse. Publication gravure printers use solvent recovery systems almost exclusively. The recovered solvent costs only a fraction of the cost of new solvent and helps to offset the cost of the solvent recovery equipment.

Solvent recovery for packaging and product gravure operations is more difficult because of the variety of solvents used in the ink and coating formulations. Recovered solvent requires further treatment before it can be reused. This often increases the cost above the cost of new solvent. Solvent recovery is very rarely cost effective for packaging and product printers running multiple solvents.

INCINERATION (THERMAL OXIDATION)

Incineration destroys high boiling solvents and other fumes that would contaminate a solvent recovery system. They can be built to accommodate a single press, and the heat from the incinerator can be reused. Energy sources for incinerators depend on the geographical location of the press. Where energy costs are a concern, incinerators equipped with a catalyst can operate at much lower temperatures. The catalysts include precious metals such as platinum and palladium. Certain materials run on the press can contaminate catalysts. When this happens, the catalyst must be replaced. The choice of incinerator must balance the initial cost of installation with the ongoing cost of operation.

Figure 7-3. Two examples of solvent recovery operations.

Low-VOC Technology

Low-VOC technology deals with pollution control by formulating the ink with as little VOCs as possible. Inks that require "curing" rather than drying fall into this category. UV inks and coatings have been very successful in flexography and rotary letterpress printing. These inks contain photoinitiators that cure when exposed to ultraviolet light, eliminating the need for any solvent capture or control. UV coatings are successfully used in gravure, but some problems still remain with pigmented inks.

Other forms of low-VOC technology include electron-beam (EB) technology, high-solids inks, and thermoplastic inks. All these technologies have been proven to have a certain degree of success in specialized applications.

We expect continued government pressure to reduce or eliminate the use of solvent in gravure operations. Gravure printers and allied industries have invested enormous amounts of capital with a great deal of success. Today's capture efficiencies exceed 98%. Water-based ink has replaced solvent ink in applications that were thought to be impossible only five years ago. We expect continued development in gravure ink technology and in equipment that will keep gravure in compliance with future regulations.

8 THE GRAVURE DOCTOR BLADE

he doctor blade is a thin flexible strip, usually of steel, that is held parallel against the surface of the gravure printing cylinder. It removes the excess ink from the smooth, unengraved surface of the cylinder allowing the ink to be retained in the recessed cells.

The action of the doctor blade is fundamental to gravure printing and has been part of the process since the 18th century. Doctor blades are also used in coating applications, flexographic printing, and paper coating.

THE DOCTOR BLADE ASSEMBLY

The doctor blade assembly is made up of the blade holder, the wiping blade, the backup blade, and the oscillation mechanism (see Figure 8.1).

The blade holder is specific to the press design. Presses intended for printing a broad range of cylinder sizes have blade holders with a wide range of adjustments. Publication and other presses that use cylinders of only a few diameters have a smaller adjustment range. In publication presses, the blade holders are fixed in the press, while in packaging and some product presses the holders are removable.

The doctor blade and backup blade, if one is being used, are inserted directly into a clamp that is part of the assembly. The holder is designed to keep the blade material flat and the edge parallel to the cylinder surface.

Figure 8.1 Example of a doctor blade assembly. (Courtesy Bobst Champlain.)

DOCTOR BLADE MATERIALS

A special, cold-rolled, hardened, and tempered strip of steel is the most commonly used material for gravure doctor blades. Several alloys are sold for doctor blades, the most popular for gravure doctor blades being electroslag refining or remelting (ESR). It is available bright polished or blue polished. There is no functional difference between the two.

If corrosion resistance is required, stainless steel blades are used. They are hardened and tempered and are more resistant to corrosion than carbon steel but not as durable. Other materials commonly used for special applications include polypropylene, Teflon, and nylon.

DOCTOR BLADE SPECIFICATIONS

Flatness and straightness are very critical for doctor blades, especially for blades exceeding 100 in. in length. Steel blade thickness varies from 0.004 in. to 0.015 in. and from less than an inch up to four inches in width. Commercial tolerances for thickness are ±0.006 mm and ±0.010 mm for width.

The backup blade is used to give the doctor blade additional support. When set up properly it creates a spring action when the doctor blade is applied to the cylinder. Stiffness can be adjusted by changing how far the doctor blade is extended beyond the backup blade. Excessive cylinder wear and premature blade wear will result if the blade setup is too stiff. If the blade setup is not stiff enough, there will be excess sensitivity to contact angle, pressure, and press speed. Backup blades are typically 0.010–0.015 in. thick.

WIPING ANGLES

Setting the blade refers to the action of bringing the doctor blade in contact with the engraved cylinder at the best angle and pressure necessary to completely wipe the excess ink from the cylinder. There are two important angles that the press operator must consider when setting a doctor blade, the set angle and the contact angle. The set angle is actually a reference angle. Some presses are equipped with instruments that can be used to achieve a pre-determined set angle. The contact angle is the net result of all the forces applied to the doctor blade when it is in operation. Manufacturers recommend a contact angle of between 55–65° for optimum wiping performance. When pressure is applied to the doctor blade at the start of the press-run, a certain amount of force is required to keep the blade in contact with the cylinder. The ink being wiped from the cylinder surface can apply hydraulic forces against the blade causing it to lift up and away from the cylinder. To alleviate this condition, some printing units are equipped with pre-wiping, non-contact blades that reduce the hydraulic pressure created on high-speed presses.

DOCTOR BLADE WEAR

ADHESIVE WEAR

Gravure inks provide the lubrication necessary to minimize blade and cylinder wear. The doctor blade actually rides on a thin film of ink. The cylinder surface is not wiped completely, but is sufficiently cleaned so that the remaining ink film will not transfer to the substrate. Adhesive wear occurs when the ink film fails to separate the blade from the cylinder.

ABRASIVE WEAR

This type of wear takes place whenever hard foreign particles are present between the blade and the engraved cylinder. Potential sources of abrasive particles include ink pigment, dried ink, rust, paper dust, particles of paper coating, doctor blade particles, and chrome flakes from the printing cylinder. Gravure ink pumping systems are equipped with filters to remove potentially abrasive materials from the ink before they can cause damage to the blade or cylinder.

One of the most common print defects unique to gravure is the doctor blade streak. Despite the many precautions taken in press design and ink handling, occasionally a foreign particle will get lodged under the doctor blade, causing a streak. Proper blade oscillation can minimize this problem and reduce cylinder wear.

Cylinder finish is also a factor in print defects. A certain amount of roughness can actually improve lubricity and doctor blade performance. The best surface finish will take into account the type of ink and solvent being used, the press speed, and the substrate. The blade-to-nip distance also affects ink transfer and must be factored into any decision dealing with doctor blade and cylinder interaction.

9 THE IMPRESSION SYSTEM

he functions of the impression roll are to force contact between the web and the engraved cylinder, to create the necessary web tension between printing units, and to propel the web through the press.

The impression roll brings the substrate in contact with the engraved cylinder resulting in proper ink transfer. It is a friction-driven, rubber-covered metal cylinder. The impression roll is not geared to the press, but is driven by friction at the nip. It helps to propel the web through the press and set the web tension pattern between press units. Impression pressure is measured in pounds per linear inch (PLI). This is the average force per inch applied over the face of the impression roller. Depending on the hardness of the roll covering and the substrate to be printed, the PLI can range from fifty to several hundred pounds.

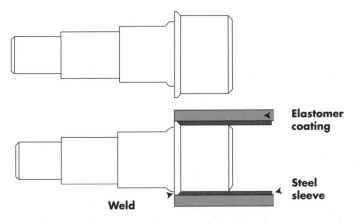

Figure 9-1. The typical impression roll consists of a tubular sleeve, supported at each end on bearings.

DESIGN

The impression roll is made of a tubular sleeve covered with a rubber compound. Roll manufacturers have a wide variety of covering materials available depending on ink and solvent type, substrate, press speed, and the use of electrostatic assist. Roll covers include natural and synthetic rubber polymers and polyurethane.

DIMENSIONS

The impression roll has two main dimensions: core diameter (the outside diameter of the metal sleeve) and outside diameter (the diameter after the rubber cover has been added to the sleeve).

BALANCE

The impression roll must be balanced to eliminate excess vibration during press operations, much the same as the construction of the image carrier cylinder. If the impression roll is out of balance, excess vibration can cause a reduction of overall mechanical efficiency, uneven impression resulting in poor print quality, excessive wear on the bearings, and uneven web tension. Excess vibration can also cause wrinkling of the substrate, heat buildup, and possible failure of the roll covering.

SPECIFICATIONS

The manufacturers of impression rollers follow the recommendations of the press manufacturer. The following specifications must be determined by the printer:

- Cover material determined by press conditions
- Hardness (shore durometer) of roll
- Physical properties of cover materials, i.e., heat resistance, resiliency, abrasion resistance, chemical resistance, and compression set
- Trim, the shape of the rubber covering at the end of the roller

ROLLER PRESSURE

During printing, the pressure of the impression roller against the cylinder forces the substrate against the engraved cylinder, causing the ink to transfer from the engraved cells to the substrate by capillary action. The press operator can adjust the pressure of the impression roller. Pressure can be varied to accommodate press type, engraving specifications, speed, ink formulation, substrate, and electrostatic assist.

THE NIP

The nip is the point of contact between the impression roller, web, and engraved printing cylinder. The pressure applied at the ends of

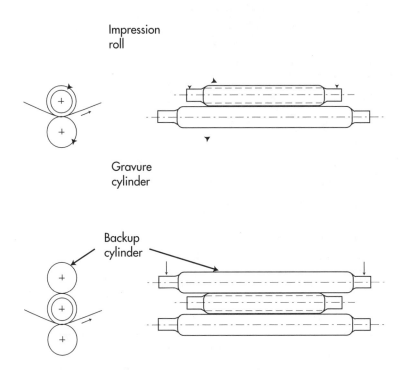

Figure 9-2. Two-roll (top) and three-roll (bottom) impression systems.

the impression roll must be distributed evenly along the entire length of the roller to create a consistent nip. The tendency of the roll to bend at its center when pressure is applied at the ends is referred to as deflection. Deflection is more likely to occur where the presses are wide (over 60 inches), cylinder circumference is small, and the press speeds are high. In other words, publication gravure and wide-web product gravure operations are subject to this problem. A number of systems have been designed to address the need for constant nip pressure. They fall into three general categories:

- Three-roller system consisting of the engraved cylinder, impression roll, and a backup roll.

    This design is limited to slower press speeds because it actually has two nips, which can create excess heat and limit the operational life of the impression roll.

- Two-roll system consisting of the engraved cylinder and a crowned impression roller.

- Two-roll system consisting of the engraved cylinder and an internally-supported impression roller.

ELECTROSTATIC ASSIST

In order for ink to transfer from the engraved cylinder, it must come in direct contact with the substrate. If the ink fails to contact the substrate, a print defect will occur. This is usually referred to as "missing dots" or "snowflaking." This condition is most likely to show up on rough substrates, particularly paper and paper board. Improving the smoothness is the obvious solution to the problem, but is not always possible or cost effective.

In 1966, the Gravure Research Institute developed a method of introducing an electric field to the nip area to help transfer ink from the engraved cylinder to the substrate. When voltage is applied across the impression roll, an electric field is generated between the impression roll and the engraved cylinder. This electric field produces an external force on the ink, pulling it toward the substrate. When the substrate leaves the nip, the charge dissipates.

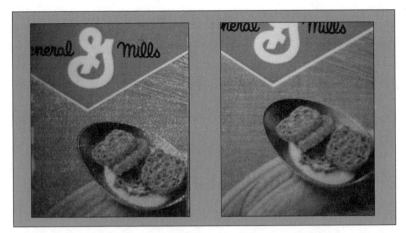

Figure 9-3. The image on the left was printed without electrostatic assist (ESA). The image on the right used ESA.

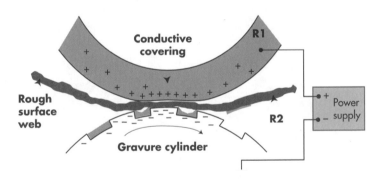

Figure 9-4. Basic schematic of the principles of electrostatic assist.

This process is called electrostatic assist (ESA). The development of ESA paved the way for ultra-high-speed presses and the ability of the gravure process to print on rough substrates with good print results.

10 SUBSTRATES

Substrates are the materials on which printing is performed. In gravure printing, substrates are divided into two categories: porous and non-porous. Ink selection, engraving specifications, and press conditions (i.e., speed, drying temperatures, tension, etc.) are all affected by the substrate to be printed.

Porous substrates are primarily paper and paperboard. Ink adheres easily to these substrates and dries by both absorption and evaporation. The Gravure Association of America classifies paper as either publication or packaging paper. Product gravure uses papers from both categories depending on the specific demands of the finished product.

PAPER TERMINOLOGY

Literally hundreds of different kinds of papers are manufactured, but very few are specifically made for gravure printing. Before discussing the various grades of paper used for gravure printing, a few definitions are necessary to understand how paper grades and weights are defined. Paper grades are classifications based upon specific measurable physical characteristics of the paper in question.

Basis weight is the weight of 500 sheets of paper that are a specific size. Most printing papers use 24×36 in. or 25×38 in. as the basis for the paper weight. Another term for this designation is "ream weight" (i.e., 24×36 in.×500 sheets equals a designated number of pounds). The most accurate and consistent way of describing paper weight is by using metric measurements that are defined as grams per square meter, eliminating the need to reference the sheet size. Most U.S. paper mills include metric measurements as well as basis weight measurements on their shipping and identification labels. Virtually all paper mills around the world use the metric system of measurement. The U.S. industry has held on to this confusing terminology that is based on paper sizes that were standard for sheetfed presses. When specifying paper, it is advisable to reference the ream size or use the metric designation to avoid any misunderstanding.

Paper board is designated by caliper rather than weight. The caliper is expressed in "points." A point equals 0.001 in. For example, a 24-pt. board is 0.024 in. thick.

Many publication and packaging papers and board are coated to improve the printing surface. Coated paper provides color, gloss, brightness, and compressibility, and it enhances the color of the printed ink. Paper coatings are made of two basic materials, pigment and binder. Binders are mixed with the pigment to hold the pigment together and help the coating to adhere to the paper. They are made from a variety of starch and/or latex products specially formulated for specific end uses. Binders used for gravure paper are generally softer than binders used for offset papers. Papers may be coated on one side (C1S) or on both sides (C2S). The coating process can be either on the paper machine or off line in a stand-alone process. The majority of gravure papers are blade-coated on the paper machine.

Another way to affect the printing surface of paper is by calendering. Calendering is a method of smoothing a web of paper and polishing its surface to a higher gloss through friction and pressure. A supercalender consists of a stack of alternating fiber-filled rolls and steel rolls. The paper is threaded through the alternating rolls. The resulting action "irons" both sides of the web to a smooth finish and high gloss. Supercalenders are equipped with steam showers to add moisture to the paper that is lost during the calendering process. Calenders that are on line with the paper machine have fewer nips than the supercalender, which is a stand-alone operation. The supercalender creates a superior paper for gravure printing. Both coated and uncoated papers can be calendered or supercalendered.

PUBLICATION PAPERS

The gravure publication industry consumes a variety of uncoated paper grades. These papers are made mostly from mechanical pulps and usually have a high bulk-to-weight ratio, high opacity, and the strength to be printed at very high speeds. Generally uncoated groundwood papers are the least expensive, lowest-quality gravure publication papers. Recent technical advances in paper manufacturing have improved the quality of these papers. There are two major types of uncoated groundwood, Roto News and supercalendered. The Gravure Association of America, in cooperation with paper manufacturers and printers, has developed a classification system for the various grades of paper in this category. Three criteria are used to define grades of uncoated roto stock (see table on the following page):

- Brightness—a measure of the paper's ability to reflect light, usually determined by measuring the reflectivity of light in selected wavelengths.
- Color—the perceived shade or hue of the paper. Most white papers have a tint of color, usually blue, yellow, or red.
- Smoothness—gravure printing requires a high level of smoothness to allow highlight and light-midtone areas to be printed without missing dots.

Smoothness can be measured on the free surface of the paper or on the surface under pressure. Because pressure is applied to the paper at the printing nip, measuring smoothness under pressure is the most accurate predictor of printability.

Standards for paper testing techniques have been developed and are available from the Technical Association of the Pulp and Paper Industry (TAPPI).

GAA ROTO NEWS CLASSIFICATIONS
(FROM LABORATORY STUDIES)

Paper Classification	Brightness	Color	Parker Print-Surface Smoothness
Group E	TAPPI 54–57	5.4–7.0% Saturation Dominant Wavelength: 575.5–578.5 Nanometers	3.6–4.4
Group D	TAPPI 55–60	5.5–7.5% Saturation Dominant Wavelength: 576–584 Nanometers	2.7–4.3
Group C	TAPPI 58–62	5.7–7.0% Saturation Dominant Wavelength: 576–577 Nanometers	2.5–3.6
Group B	TAPPI 64–65	5.0% Saturation Dominant Wavelength: 575 Nanometers	2.5–2.9
Group A	TAPPI 64–65	2.5–4.5% Saturation Dominant Wavelength: 572–578 Nanometers	3.6–4.4

Roto News basis weights are expressed in terms of a 24×36 in.× 500-sheet ream and range from 25 to 32 pounds. These papers are typically used in gravure-printed newspaper supplements, weekly magazines, newspaper advertising inserts, and, to a lesser extent, catalogs.

During the late 1980s and early 1990s a new finishing technology called "soft-nip" calendering was developed and installed on many paper machines. This type of calendering involved running a web of paper through a series of nips consisting of one hard metal roll and one soft covered roll. The hard metal roll can be heated. By varying the temperature and the nip pressures, a wide range of printability characteristics can be developed.

Supercalendered (SC) uncoated groundwood paper resembles Roto News in may ways, but it contains a higher percentage of bleached chemical pulp and large amounts of filler pigments. SC papers are stronger, brighter, and generally produce higher print quality than Roto News papers. SC papers range in basis weight from 28 to 50 pounds on a 25×38 in.×500-sheet ream.

SC papers are labeled SC-B or SC-A to indicate levels of brightness, smoothness, and gloss. The newest gravure supercalendered grade, SC-A+, is the result of a development in papermaking technology. This grade has superior ink holdout and printability with gloss levels and smoothness close to those available in coated papers.

COATED PAPERS

Coated papers fall into two major categories, groundwoods and freesheets. They are generally more expensive than uncoated papers and are preferred for high-quality publications.

Coated groundwood grades include ultralightweight coated (ULWC), lightweight coated (LWC), mediumweight coated (MWC), and heavyweight coated (HWC). ULWC papers are typically 32 pounds or less. LWC papers can go up to 40 pounds, and MWC and HWC papers are over 40 pounds. These weights are based on a 25×38 in.×500-sheet ream.

The highest quality and most expensive papers used in publication gravure are coated freesheets. They are commonly used in high-end commercial printing applications such as catalogs, magazines, and annual reports. These papers are usually purchased in higher basis weights than the groundwood papers. The basis weights range from 35 to 100 pounds in a 25×38 in.×500-sheet ream. The brightness range for a coated free sheet is from 76 to 90.

PACKAGING PAPERS

Most of the papers used in packaging gravure fall into three categories: uncoated, supercalendered, and coated papers. Most papers sold for gravure package printing are considered specialty grades. They are almost always made to order, as opposed to being shipped from a paper mill or merchant's inventory.

Uncoated papers are made without any surface treatment other than surface sizing. They are used in applications where there is simple line work and no demanding graphic reproduction is required.

Supercalendered papers are usually smoother and denser than uncoated papers and can be suitable for halftone reproduction. Supercalendered publication grade papers are used in various product gravure applications including some grades of giftwrap.

The most commonly used papers in gravure packaging printing are coated papers. Both C1S and C2S papers are used. The heavier basis weights are usually supercalendered to improve the printing surface. Along with the necessary smoothness, brightness, gloss, and color, packaging papers often require a number of physical properties necessary for the performance demands of the end product. Some of the properties include crack and heat resistance, opacity, mold resistance, moisture resistance, oil and grease resistance, and other barrier properties.

Label papers have a variety of packaging applications. Basis weights range from 40 to 80 pounds on a 25×38 in.×500-sheet ream size. These papers are usually coated on one side. The clay-coated surface is either supercalendered or coated with multiple lightweight layers of coating to produce a smooth glossy finish. The back side of the paper is usually sized during the papermaking process to reduce the paper's tendency to curl in the printing, finishing, and subsequent packaging applications. Specific coating formulations have been developed for gravure label papers to enhance print performance and converting.

Uncoated papers, with either a machine glaze or machine finish are used in label applications where heat is involved, reducing the possibility of blistering. These applications most often fall into the category of heat-seal papers. Uncoated papers are also used in a variety of laminated structures.

PAPERBOARD

In general, all paper that is thicker than 12 points (0.012 in.) is classified as paperboard. As in all paper and graphic arts terminology, there are quite a few exceptions to this definition. Paperboard like paper is available in a variety of grades, including coated, uncoated, and those containing recycled fiber. Paperboard is available in a variety of thickness or caliper. Each caliper has a typical corresponding basis weight. Basis weight for paperboard is measured as pounds per thousand square feet.

Solid bleached sulfate (SBS) is made from 100% bleached virgin pulp. It is a solid white board that is usually coated on one side to improve printability. SBS has a smoother, more consistent surface than other paperboards. It is widely used in food packaging, cosmetics, and pharmaceuticals.

Unbleached board, also called natural kraft, is used either coated or uncoated and offers a variety of characteristics for specialized product needs.

Recycled paperboard is often manufactured from recycled materials. It is known by a number of different names including combination boxboard and cylinder board. This board is used extensively for folding cartons including detergent cartons, cereal cartons, and tissue cartons, to name a few.

Recycled paperboard is made on a cylinder paper machine and is manufactured in layers. The raw materials used in each layer can be different. The printing surface is clay coated and calendered for good print reproduction. The backside of the board may be gray, brown, or white depending on the recycled materials used to manufacture the board. The appearance of recycled paperboard can vary among manufacturers.

NONPOROUS SUBSTRATES

Plastics make up the largest group of nonporous substrates, followed by plastic-coated substrates, foil, foil laminations, and metallized paper. Most plastics used in gravure printing, with the exception of sheet vinyl, are thin films either unsupported or as part of a composite structure called a lamination. These films include:

- Polyethylene
- Polypropylene
- Polyvinyl chloride (PVC)
- Polyethylene terephthalate (PET)
- Polyester
- Polystyrene

Other substrates in this category include:
- Cellophane
- Nylon
- Metallized polypropylene
- Metallized polyester
- Coated paper

For gravure printing, the surface of these substrates requires special preparation to insure good ink adhesion. Films have inherently low surface energy levels and behave in much the same way as glass when a liquid is deposited on them. This condition is referred to as wettability. In order for the ink to adequately wet the substrate, the surface tension of the ink must be lower than the surface energy of the substrate. Both the ink and the substrate can be treated to achieve this balance.

Surface treatment of the substrate is usually done in-line when the film is being manufactured and the process is most efficient. Treatment can also be applied in-line with laminating and printing.

The most common treatment done in-line on a gravure press is corona treatment. It involves a high-voltage discharge and ionization of the air in the space above the moving web, causing ozone to form. Ozone is a powerful oxidizing agent, and degrades the film surface, creating a surface area that ink can adhere to.

PLASTIC COATINGS

PVDC coatings are used to improve the appearance and barrier properties of many packaging substrates. PVDC is a copolymer that is mixed with other monomers in proportions that are designed for a specific end use, such as laminating adhesive, top coat, or primer. PVDC can be formulated for flexibility, elongation, resistance to blocking, grease resistance, and moisture and vapor barriers.

Several methods can be used to apply PVDC coatings depending on the substrate and equipment available. Reverse roll coaters, air knife coaters, and wire-wound rod coaters are commonly used. These coatings are used on paper, glassine, polypropylene, polyester, polyethylene, and nylon. Packaging applications include snack foods, dairy products, meat, and pharmaceutical packaging. In addition to barrier properties, PVDC coatings also provide heat seal, grease resistance, solvent resistance, abrasion resistance, gloss, and flame retardance. PVDC-coated substrates are not usually stable in freeze-thaw conditions.

METALLIZED SUBSTRATES

Metallizing is the process of vaporizing a metal and depositing it on a substrate in a vacuum chamber. Metallizing is not limited to substrates and has a variety of industrial applications. In packaging, aluminum is the metal most often used. It is inexpensive and easy to vaporize and produces a bright, stable coating. Metallized films and papers require surface treatment to insure ink, coating, and adhesive bonding. The treatment depends on the substrate and the end use.

Metallized substrates include polyester, polypropylene, polycarbonate, cellophane, paper, paperboard, and fabric. Packaging applications include coffee bags, cosmetics, candy and cigarette wrappers, snack food bags, poultry, nuts, and pet food as well as photographic supplies. Decorative applications include auto trim, balloons, giftwrap, and wall covering.

ALUMINUM FOIL AND FOIL LAMINATIONS

Aluminum foil is not only a very attractive packaging substrate, but it is also an absolute barrier to gas, moisture and light, prolonging product shelf life. Foil can be coated with a variety of substances for use with products that might corrode the foil. Foil can also be used in an endless variety of laminations that include paper, films, and adhesives.

Aluminum foil requires priming for good ink adhesion. Typical primers include shellac, acrylic, nitrocellulose, and vinyl. Foil also requires special attention on press to insure proper ink drying, tension, and mechanical considerations such as smooth rollers to avoid scuffing or distorting the foil surface.

11 INKS AND SOLVENTS

nk is the critical link that ties the mechanical parts of the printing process together. Gravure inks are fluid, fast drying, and functional for virtually any application that can be produced on a gravure press.

Gravure ink is made of colorant dispersed in a vehicle capable of forming a very thin continuous film. After printing, the ink dries by evaporation leaving a dry printed film. Gravure inks can be custom-formulated for different substrates and end uses.

INK COMPOSITION

Ink compositions include colorants and vehicles. Vehicles are composed of binders, modifiers, and solvents.

COLORANT

The component that imparts color to ink by absorbing selected wavelengths of light is a pigment or a dye. Pigments are fine solid particles that are insoluble in the liquid portion of the ink. They are selected for properties such as color, lightfastness, and chemical resistance. Dyes are soluble in the liquid portion of the ink and can be either synthetic or natural in origin. Most dyes are very transparent and have limited resistance properties. Fluorescent inks are made from dyes.

VEHICLES

Vehicles are made up of binders, modifiers, and solvents. *Binders* act as the glue that keeps the colorant and other ingredients evenly dispersed in the liquid ink and adhere it to the substrate. The main component of the binder is the resin, a special class of polymers that may be either natural or synthetic. The resin is dissolved in a solvent along with other components of the vehicle. After printing, the solvent evaporates in a process of drying and the resin solidifies. The remaining solid layer of resin, colorant, and other ingredients is called the ink film. Common resins include nitrocellulose, maleics, phenolics, vinyl co-polymers, modified rosin esters, and acrylics.

Modifiers are added during ink manufacturing to improve such properties as holdout, gloss, and scuff resistance. Modifiers, also referred to as additives, perform a very important function and can determine the success or failure of gravure ink. Modifiers added during the formulation process include neutral pigments, waxes, plasticizers, viscosity modifiers, and slip agents.

Solvent serves two purposes: to dissolve the resin and to adjust viscosity. Solvent is classified as either active, diluent, cosolvent, or incompatible, based on its ability to dissolve the resin in a specific ink. A solvent for one resin system may be incompatible in another. Active solvent is a true solvent for the ink resins. A diluent thins ink without acting on the resin. Cosolvents are mixtures of solvents that are more active mixed together than they are separately. Incompatible solvents will not mix with the ink formula and can cause the ink system to degrade. For example, an incompatible solvent added in a very small amount can cause resin to kick out of the ink. Technically this is the flocculation or precipitation of the solid part of an ink.

INK MANUFACTURING

The majority of gravure printers purchase inks manufactured to suit their needs. Some printers purchase what they call bases and blend their own finished ink. A base is a highly pigmented dispersion that is made and stored separately from a finished ink. Blending is the process of custom-mixing the pigment dispersion with the vehicle, solvent, and modifiers to form a stable ink ready for printing or shipping. Either way, the physical properties and performance characteristics must be built into the ink from the very beginning of the process.

The goal of the ink manufacturer is to minimize the press-side adjustments needed during a pressrun. Gravure inks are manufactured strong so they can be thinned and extended to compensate for the following:

- Cylinder wear
- Variations in the substrate
- Variations from press to press
- Variations in doctor blade settings
- Variations in press speeds
- Changes in drying rates caused by atmospheric conditions

DISPERSION

Dispersion is a complicated process consisting of three overlapping steps: wetting, grinding, and stabilization. The dispersion is created by uniformly distributing the pigment particles in a vehicle.

During wetting, the air on the surface of the pigment particles is displaced by the vehicle components. The grinding step breaks aggregates or agglomerates of pigment into smaller particles. Grinding is accomplished using a heavy-duty machine called a mill. A variety of mills are used for pigment grinding.

Stabilization of a dispersion is necessary to prevent the pigment particles from re-agglomerating or flocculating. Flocculation can cause a loss of color, lower gloss, poor rub resistance, and increased settling in storage.

PROPERTIES OF INKS AND EXTENDERS

In addition to viscosity (covered earlier in this book), gravure inks have several properties that influence the flow of the ink. Fluids that have the same viscosity, no matter how fast they are flowing or how vigorously they are agitated, are called Newtonian fluids. Water and motor oil are good examples of Newtonian fluids.

Fluids that change in viscosity when agitated are called non-Newtonian fluids. Most gravure inks fall into this category. The presence of pigments and other solids causes the ink to have a higher viscosity when at rest than when in motion. Different types of pumps can be used on the ink delivery system on a gravure press to reduce the mechanical effects on the fluid ink.

The tendency of ink viscosity to drop when the ink is agitated and then immediately return to a state of higher viscosity within seconds after agitation is stopped is called thixotropy. This is a common property of water-based inks and some solvent-based publication inks. Understanding the behavior of these fluids is necessary for the printer to efficiently maintain optimum printing viscosity.

COLOR

Strength or intensity of color is an important characteristic of gravure ink. There are three types of instruments commonly used to measure color—colorimeters, densitometers, and spectrophotometers. Understanding the difference between these instruments is important for proper communication between the printer, print buyer, and ink manufacturer.

The colorimeter or filter spectrophotometer views a sample through three wide-band color filters. These filters mimic the human eye's sensitivity to red, green, and blue light. This is a handy pressroom tool, especially for checking line or solid colors. It is used in packaging and product gravure more often than in publication gravure.

Densitometers are very useful for determining the amount of ink on a substrate. They do not match the human eye's sensitivity to color, and they are not able to detect differences in color. Densitometers are used primarily for process-color printing.

Spectrophotometers measure the relative energy levels, or intensities, of all the visible wavelengths reflected or transmitted from a sample. The measurements can be used to produce a three-dimensional graph of an individual color. The spectrophotometer is capable of translating color differences into a set of coordinates representing positions in a color space system such as CIE L*a*b*.

The appearance of color is influenced by the viewing conditions which include the light source, the surroundings, and the viewer. Noon sunlight from a slightly overcast sky has a flat distribution curve (i.e., the light is neutral white with no predominant hue). By comparison, incandescent light has a predominant red and yellow hue, and fluorescent light is predominantly blue. The viewing field of the surround influences the viewer. Because the light source and viewing conditions exert a strong influence on color perception, color comparisons should be made under standardized conditions, with a neutral gray surround and a 5000 K light source set at an overhead angle to eliminate shadows.

Color measurement instruments have many practical applications. They can be used to compare incoming materials to standards, and cylinder proofs to production proofs. Color measurement instruments can also be mounted on the press to monitor color during the printing process.

INK CLASSIFICATION

The Gravure Association of America has developed an ink classification system over the years to assist the printer in determining the proper solvent to use for mixing. In publication gravure, the letter designations are rarely used today. In an attempt to set standards for communication, the Gravure Publication Ink Committee set up basic classifications in which the inks are classified by end use. Group I inks are designed for tabloids, supplements, magazines, and inserts printed on uncoated groundwoods and SC-B papers. Group VI / SWOP inks are formulated primarily for coated paper. SWOP is the "Specifications for Web Offset Printing." The GAA ink classification system is still used for packaging and product inks.

- A-type inks use aliphatic hydrocarbons as solvent. These are usually used for publication printing and can be referred to as Group VII inks.

- B-type inks are also publication inks and usually require at least 50% of the solvent to be an aromatic hydrocarbon. These inks are also referred to as Group VI.
- C-type inks include various formulations, most of which contain nitrocellulose. These formulations require solvents of the ester or ketone class such as ethyl acetate, isopropyl acetate, or normal propyl acetate, acetone, or methyl ethyl ketone (MEK). These solvents can be mixed with alcohol because alcohol is a latent solvent for nitrocellulose; when mixed with an equal amount of an acetate solvent, alcohol works as well as a pure ester. C-type inks are the most common solvent-based inks used in packaging gravure.

There are eleven categories in the GAA ink classifications. In addition, there are special inks and coatings that are not classified. Many special coatings have been developed to enhance end use performance. Some of these products include catalytic coatings, barrier coatings, ultraviolet cured coatings (UV), and heat transfer inks for textile decorating. The Food and Drug Administration (FDA) and the United States Department of Agriculture (USDA) set regulations that affect the choice of pigments and vehicles that can be used to formulate inks for specific applications. Gravure printers and print buyers need to be aware of any regulations that might affect a particular application.

SPECIAL PRODUCTS

As mentioned earlier, the gravure printing process has the ability to handle many unique products. Listed below are just a few of these applications.

- Heat-seal coatings resemble a clear transparent topcoat. During a subsequent converting operation such as bag making, the heat seal will remelt and fuse with itself or some other surface of the package.

Figure 11-1. Ink drawdown test.

- Cold-seal adhesives have the ability to adhere to themselves, making a seal without using heat. This is especially useful for ice cream and other frozen products.
- Laminating adhesives can be applied either in line on a gravure press or on a laminating machine. The laminating adhesive provides a bond between two substrates and contributes barrier properties to the structure.
- Electrically conductive coatings are usually pigmented with conductive carbon black. One use for this coating is as a background for spark discharge graph papers and message forms.

INK TESTS AND MEASUREMENTS

WET INK TESTS

The most important test to perform before using ink on press is a test for color, shade, and strength. This is easily accomplished with a drawdown. Drawdowns from the ink to be used should be compared to an existing standard. To insure the tests produce predictable and reliable results, consistent procedures, equipment, and viewing conditions should always be used. Ink drawdowns can be made using a smooth-edged blade, wire-wound rod, glass rod, or a laboratory proof press. Other wet ink tests include:

- Ink viscosity should be measured after the ink has been thoroughly mixed and is at pressroom temperature.
- Test pH for the acidity or alkalinity of the ink. Water-based inks in particular should be tested for proper pH levels. A pH meter is the most reliable method of testing.
- Ink abrasiveness can be tested on a variety of abrasion testers. Abrasive ink can cause excessive cylinder and doctor blade wear.
- Weight per gallon should be checked on each new batch of ink when it is received. The reading should be taken at a standard temperature, since ink is subject to volume expansion when heated. Fluid ink is sold by the pound and delivered by the gallon.
- Solids content is related to weight per gallon. Solids are what is left after the ink is completely dry. Solids content is very important in determining coat weight and engraving specifications.

TESTS FOR PRINTED SUBSTRATE

Printed products must meet customer specifications for both appearance and performance. Physical tests are conducted to insure product performance. Visual tests are used to evaluate the printed product for print defects and correct color match.

Physical tests include:

- Rub or abrasion is common to all gravure-printed products. The Sutherland rub tester is widely used to test for rub resistance and the Tabor tester is commonly used for abrasion testing.
- Blocking is a condition wherein the printed surface adheres to itself and another surface. It is a function of temperature, relative humidity, pressure, time, and the surface characteristics of the contact material. Many blocking tests have been developed to predict a printed product's tendency to block.
- Slip refers to coefficient of friction (COF). COF is an extremely important property for publications and packaging convert-

ing. There is a variety of testing equipment available, but results are difficult to correlate. Standard test methods should be established between the printer and customer to insure consistent product performance.

- Ink adhesion is usually tested with a 6-in. strip of Scotch #600 or 610 adhesive tape. It is pressed firmly against the ink film, with a short tab free for grasping. The tape is quickly pulled or lifted at approximately 45°. The amount of ink transferred to the tape is evaluated. Variations to this test have been established to meet specific end-use requirements.

Other visual tests include:
- Register
- Skipping or missing dots
- Mottle
- Drag-out
- Haze
- Setoff
- Picking
- Pinholing
- Railroading or tracks
- Screening
- Scumming
- Snowflaking
- Volcano
- Whiskering and feathering

Complete descriptions of print defects and test methods are available from the Gravure Association of America.

12 PREPRESS FOR GRAVURE

I n order to print color images, the basic colors in the original image have to be separated. Originals can be photographs, artwork, or digital files. Varying values approximating the amount of ink needed to reproduce the original image represents each of the basic colors, yellow, magenta, cyan, and black. Corrections to these color separations, re-touching, and the composition of the final page or image layout are carried out on prepress computer systems. Digital data is then supplied to gravure engraving machines.

Each printing process has its limitations, and gravure is no exception. Ideally, the designer should be aware of the elements that contribute to a printable product. Presses are not perfect, and substrates have variations. For example, the dimensional stability of the substrate should always be taken into account when close register is required, especially in packaging. Other factors to consider include the number of ink stations either available or required and the type of ink required.

Desktop publishing and electronic editing systems enable designers, advertising agencies, printers, and publishers to take full advantage of gravure's ability to operate in a totally digital environment. Direct digital engraving (engraving without the use of film), has been a reality since 1980. The potential speed of this technology places new emphasis on the quality of communication among buyers, agencies, engravers, and printers.

Today gravure prepress is virtually a generic process. Gravure uses the same standard data formats for input that are used for offset lithography. All publication, packaging, and product gravure operations are capable of a total digital workflow. When film is used, it is mostly used as an approval medium. What remains unique about gravure is the ability to electronically manage the output data to the engraving machine. This provides the capability to maximize engraving quality for specific inks and substrates. Since the image carrier is very stable and ink is transferred directly from the gravure engraving to the substrate, the printed product is very consistent throughout the print production run.

The GAA Input Specifications for Publication Gravure uses SWOP as a standard reference for color. Colorimetric Specifications for Publication Proofing and Printing have been developed by the GAA Colorimetric Task Force. These terms of reference appear on the following pages. The GAA language was recently adopted by the International Standards Organization (ISO) for international colorimetric standards.

In addition to publication standards, a booklet of guidelines titled *Production Ready Electronic Files for Packaging*, designed to assist packaging clients in preparing digital files for package printing is available from the GAA. The packaging guidelines are also compatible with the prepress requirements for product gravure.

One word of caution must be mentioned here, it is imperative that the client, printer, and prepress supplier communicate to avoid unnecessary time-consuming and costly errors in the preparation of art and copy for reproduction.

GRAVURE ASSOCIATION OF AMERICA INPUT SPECIFICATIONS FOR PUBLICATION GRAVURE
Revised November 1996

The GAA Specifications for Publication Gravure are intended for advertising production in magazines and other publications where supplied halftone film or electronic files are the inputs for reproduction. These specifications apply to both coated and uncoated stocks. The degree to which the final gravure printed reproduction matches the brightness, print smoothness, and gloss of the color guide will be determined by the printing stock of the publication. The GAA specifications for halftone films to be used for gravure printing are virtually identical to the SWOP specifications for offset printing. For this reason, the GAA has adopted SWOP® specifications as the basis for supplied ad materials to be used in gravure publication printing. Today, many publications successfully utilize both gravure and offset printing in the production of their magazines by adhering to the following GAA specifications.

COLORS
Gravure standard colors are to match the SWOP® colors hereafter referred to as GAA/SWOP®. The standard reference for these colors is the SWOP® standard. Colorimetric data for these references is available through the GAA.

COLOR GUIDANCE
Offset press proofs or off-press proofs may be supplied as color guidance for gravure printing.

Press Proofs   Made to SWOP® specifications for offset proofing.
Off-press Proofs Made to the manufacturer's application data sheet specific for SWOP printing conditions.

PROOFING STOCK

Current SWOP® standard or equivalent.

Press Proofs   60-lb. Champion Textweb

Off-press Proofs   Follow manufacturer's specifications stated in their
                     application data sheet which should be similar in
                     hue and brightness to 60-lb. Champion Textweb.
                     Glossy finishes are not recommended. Matte fin-
                     ishes are preferred.

FILM SPECIFICATIONS

Positive right-reading, emulsion-down 0.004-in. thick film. Scales,
target patterns, and other control devices included with the film are
to be specified by SWOP®. All type and line art, reverse and surprinting, should be provided as separate pieces of film.

SCREEN RULINGS

GAA standards are 133-line minimum. Materials provided which are
coarser than 133-line are to be handled in accordance with agree-
ment among the involved advertising agency, the publisher, and the
publisher's printer.

SCREEN ANGLES

Materials can be provided at any angles as long as moiré patterns
are avoided. Experience with halftone input shows that colors other
than yellow should avoid angles between 75 and 105°.

TOTAL AREA COVERAGE

The maximum TAC of any one square inch spot or larger in the
four colors should be no more than 300%, and only one color may
be a solid. (300% TAC is not a limiting factor for gravure printing,
and on uncoated stocks a higher TAC may be preferred.)

GRAY COMPONENT REPLACEMENT/UNDERCOLOR ADDITION

The use of GCR must be accompanied by the appropriate amount
of UCA to assure that sufficient strength is maintained in dark gray

and black areas of an image. If the appropriate amount of UCA is not applied, the contrast of an image will be reduced. See the following table for minimum three-color UCA relationships.

Due to the reduced opacity and increased porosity of uncoated stocks, GCR applications may not be suitable for all users. Therefore, the use of GCR on uncoated stocks is a matter to be resolved and pre-approved by all parties involved.

MINIMUM TAC FOR GCR		
Black Printer Dot Percentage	Minimum Three-Color Area Coverage	
	Coated Paper	Uncoated Paper
98	100	125
95	120	145
90	165	180
85	190	195
80	210	210
75	220	220
70	230	230

Notes:
The values in this table are based on the densities of the single-color black being within 10% of a three-color overprint black.
The three-color balance (cyan, magenta, and yellow) remaining in dark gray colors after GCR is applied must remain neutral gray.

CRITICAL IMAGE AREAS

Halftone films suitable for offset publication printing will be suitable for gravure publication printing. To assure good tone reproduction, the edges of cuts and other image areas intended to be distinctly visible from the paper to be printed on should be a minimum of 5% in the weakest component color.

TYPE REPRODUCTION SPECIFICATIONS AND GUIDELINES

Fine type and line art. Fine serifs, small lettering, and thin line art should be avoided. Medium and small type and thin line art should be restricted to a single process color.

Surprinting type and line art. Surprinting type should not be less than 0.004-in. at the thinnest part of a character or rule. The surrounding tone value must be light enough (<30%) to assure legibility.

Reverse type and line art. Reverse type and line art should not be less than 0.007-in. at the thinnest part of a character or rule. In addition, the subordinate colors must be spread/swelled to minimize register variation and optimize legibility in the final printed product. The surrounding tone must be dark enough to assure legibility.

Legibility. It is difficult to specify in words when, or when not to, surprint or reverse type overprinting tone. Experience has proven that it is best for all concerned if all type and line art are incorporated into the color guide and approved by the advertiser.

FILM INSPECTION

Supplied film should be inspected in accordance with the SWOP film inspection form and procedures.

ELECTRONIC FILES

Electronic files are widely accepted and in many cases are the preferred input for gravure publication printing and their use is encouraged. However, the use of electronic files should still be pre-approved by all parties involved and be in conformance with the most current ANSI and ISO standards.

It is recommended that users adhere to the following: the exchange of digital information between different imaging systems should be in accordance with the GAA-endorsed ANSI and ISO standards. (Digital data exchange specifications ANSI IT8.8 TIFF/IT).

GLOSSARY OF TERMS

AGGLOMERATE   Undispersed particles that form into a cluster.

AGGREGATE   A chain of undispersed particles or clusters.

ANGLE BAR   A metal bar or roll used either singly or in succession to re-orient the web direction.

BALANCING   The redistribution of mass to make it more evenly distributed throughout.

BALLARD SHELL   A thin skin of copper plated separately over the surface of a base cylinder. The base cyclinder is ground and polished before treatment with one of several liquid parting agents, which prevent the copper layer from bonding directly to the base surface. The copper skin may be engraved and used for printing, after which it is easily stripped from the base cylinder; a new copper skin may be plated onto the base cylinder after the cylinder has been retreated with a parting agent.

BARRIER COATING   The coating applied to a substrate to make it resistant to the passage of moisture vapor, gases, water, or other liquids including oils.

BASIS WEIGHT   The weight of 500 sheets (one ream) of any paper in its given basis size. Newsprint weights are based on a 24×36-in. sheet, other publication grades on a 25×38-in. sheet.

BINDER   The adhesive component, or components, of an ink, normally supplied by the resin formulation.

BLOCKING   The sticking together of a printed surface and another surface brought into contact through stacking or rewinding.

CALENDER   A stack or series of iron rollers that press a web of paper during papermaking into a smoother, more uniform surface. Calendering may also be performed off-machine.

CALIPER   The thickness of paper, measured with a micrometer.

CARBON TISSUE   Light-sensitive material attached to gravure cylinders, used as a resist in the chemical etching process. It consists of layers of gelatin, dye, photosensitive material, and a paper or plastic backing. Exposed to a screen and a continuous-tone image, carbon tissue permits the etching of cells of variable depth according to the degree of exposure in each cell area. Until the advent of electronic engraving, the predominant method of imaging a cylinder.

CATALYST   A substance that makes possible or enhances a chemical reaction, but which is not consumed in the reaction. Catalysts are added in various chemical processes (plating, ink drying) and are engineered, where possible, to be continually reused as other materials are removed and replenished.

CATALYTIC COATING   Coatings formulated as two-part systems, available in both water- and solvent-reducible formulas. They use reactive resins that cure to form a thermoset film. They have heat and abrasion resistance, high gloss, solvent resistance, and adhere to a wide variety of substrates.

COEFFICIENT OF FRICTION   The ratio of the frictional force resisting movement of the surface being tested to the force applied normal to that surface (the weight of the material above that surface).

COLD SEAL   An adhesive product that can be applied on a gravure press. The adhesive only adheres to itself and is usually printed in a registered pattern. It is most commonly used for frozen confectionary packaging.

COLORANT   The color portion of an ink, may be a pigment, dye or combination of the two.

CONTINUOUS TONE   Term used to describe any camera or scanner input material that has varying tones of gray formed by the grain pattern of a photographic emulsion, made without the use of screens or dots. All traditional photographs (prints and transparencies) are continuous-tone materials.

CORONA TREATMENT   A high-voltage discharge and ionization of the air in the space above the moving web, causing ozone to form. The ozone, a powerful oxidizing agent, affects the surface of the substrate, improving the ability of inks and coatings to adhere it.

CREASING   The folding of a sheet material without the appearance in the zone of folding cracks, sharp lines of bending failure, splitting away of surface coating, or other unsightly manifestations of fractures. This should be carefully distinguished from brittleness, as the latter involves a small degree of bending.

CYLINDER   Rollers in the printing press upon which the rubber plates are mounted and which receive the impressions.

DEFLOCCULATE   To disperse pigment clusters into smaller units in an ink; the reverse of flocculate.

DIECUT   The use of sharp steel rules to cut special shapes, boxes and containers, from printed sheets. Diecutting can be done on either flatbed or rotary presses. Rotary diecutting is usually inline with the printing.

DIRECT TRANSFER   A method of transferring an image directly from film to metal, exposing a resist-coated cylinder directly through the film. This method was introduced in the 1950s as a replacement for carbon tissue.

DOCTOR BLADE   Thin, flexible steel blade that passes over a gravure plate or cylinder, wiping off excess ink before an impression is made on paper. Can also refer to the entire assembly consisting of blade, doctor blade holder, and all necessary adjusting and loading devices.

DOCTOR BLADE STREAK   Defect caused by the doctor blade not wiping clean, leaving stripes or lines of color on the web.

DUROMETER   A measure of rubber hardness usually made with Shore-A durometer gauge.

DWELL TIME   The time interval during which elements remain in contract or in a static position; pause.

DYNAMIC BALANCE   Ability of special equipment to run in perfect balance at high speed.

EFFLUX CUP   A simple viscometer such as the Zahn, Shell, or Hiccup; gauges viscosity readings rapidly in terms of the number of seconds required for the cup to empty through an orifice of known size.

ELECTROPLATING   The electrodeposition of an adherent metallic coating on an electrode for the purpose of securing a surface with properties or dimensions different from those of base metal.

ELECTROSTATIC ASSIST (ESA)   A method of applying a high-voltage, low-amperage charge to the gravure impression roll, which significantly improves ink transfer during printing to minimize print defects such as skipping and snowflaking.

ETCH   To dissolve unevenly a part of the surface of a metal using an acid or other corrosive substance.

FESTOON   A method of inline storing of paper during printing, which uses a set of rollers that separate.

FLEXOGRAPHY   A method of direct rotary printing using resilient raised-image printing plates, affixed to variable repeat plate cylinders, inked by a roll or doctor-blade-wiped anilox roll carrying fluid ink.

FLOCCULATE   To aggregate pigment particles in the ink to form clusters or chains; may result in a loss of color strength and a change in hue.

GRAIN DIRECTION   Direction in which most fibers lie, corresponding with the direction the paper is made on the paper machine

HALFTONE   The reproduction of continuous-tone artwork, such as a photograph, through a crossline or contact screen, which converts the image into dots of various sizes.

HAZARDOUS AIR POLLUTANT (HAP)   According to law, a pollutant to which no ambient air quality standard is applicable and that may cause or contribute to an increase in mortality or in serious illness. For example, asbestos, beryllium, and mercury have been declared HAPs.

HEAT SEAL   A method of uniting two or more surfaces by fusion, either the coatings or the base materials, under controlled conditions of temperature, pressure, and time (dwell).

IMAGE CARRIER   Any plate, form, cylinder, or other surface which contains an image, receives ink, and transfers it to another surface, e.g., gravure cylinders, offset plates, and letterpress stereotypes.

IMPOSITION   Laying out pages in a press form so that they will be in the correct order after the printed sheet is folded.

IMPRESSION ROLLER   A friction-driven, rubber-covered metal cylinder that squeezes the substrate against an inked, engraved cylinder on a gravure press.

INTAGLIO   Any printing process using a recessed image carrier. Refers to fine art copperplate printing from etchings; commercial copperplate "engraving" used for business cards, stationery, stamps and security printing; and all sheetfed and rotogravure printing. Generally used in an historical context, and to distinguish gravure from other processes, the term is falling into general disuse in the commercial sector of the industry.

INTEGRAL SHAFT   A cylinder base design in which the supporting shaft is permanently attached to the printing cylinder.

LETTERPRESS   A method of printing that uses a relief plate as an image carrier. The image area of the plate, raised above the non-printing area, receives ink from rollers, and transfers it directly to the substrate being printed.

LITHOGRAPHY   A method of printing from a plane surface (as a smooth stone or metal plate) on which the image to be printed is ink-receptive and the non-printing area is ink repellent.

MANDREL   Cylinder that is not permanently mounted on a shaft and can be removed.

MODIFIER   A material added to the basic ink formulation to improve the behavior of the ink on the press, or to improve the characteristics of the ink film. Often used interchangeably with additive.

MORDANT   A substance that, when applied to fiber in conjunction with a dye, causes increased dye fixation.

NIP   Line of contact between two rolls.

ORGANIC DYE   A general classification of pigments that are carbon-based, as opposed to metallic pigments.

PHOTO INITIATOR   An additive in ultraviolet curable inks and coatings that acts as a catalyst when the ink or coating is exposed to ultraviolet light.

PRINTED GLOSS   Reflection of brightness or luster from a printed surface.

REEL STAND   Device at the unwind section of the press that holds the reel (roll) of substrate to be printed. Also called the unwind stand.

RESIN   A complex organic substance which, in solvent solution, forms the gravure varnish; after drying, resins become the binder, or film-forming materials.

RESIST (n.)   (1) Material that resists the action of a plating solution. (2) Materials applied to part of a cathode or plating rack to render it non-conductive.

REVERSE PRINTING UNIT   A printing deck on a gravure press that reverses the web path without turning it, allowing the back (reverse) of the substrate to be printed.

REWINDING   The process of rewinding a roll of paper to produce a proper size for the customer, to splice the ends together, and/or to remove defects.

RIBBON   The slit portions of the full web on a publication press. The web is slit into ribbons before the paper enters the next section of the folder for processing.

ROTOGRAVURE   An intaglio printing (q.v.) process for rotary web presses.

RUB   In printing, an ink that has not reached maximum dryness and does mar with normal abrasion.

SCREEN PRINTING   A printing process that employs stencils adhered to tighly drawn screens. Ink is forced through the openings in the stencil and onto the substrate. This process is well suited for printing on materials like glass, wood, thick plastics, and textiles.

SIGNATURE   In printing and binding, the name given to a printed sheet after it has been folded.

SIZING   Resins, starches or other compounds added to paper to increase its resistance to penetration by ink and water. Paper with little sizing, such as newsprint is called slack-sized; heavily-sized papers such as bond and ledger are called hard-sized. Sizing may be mixed in the pulp or applied to the surface of a partially-dry web (surface-sized).

SLEEVE Tubular part of a base cylinder, which can be mounted on a shaft.

SLIP An ink additive that imparts lubricating qualities to the surface of the dried ink film.

SLITTING Cutting printed sheets or webs into two or more sections by means of cutting wheels on a press or folder.

SOLVENT Liquid that dissolves a solid. In ink, the evaporation of solvent leaves the solids behind as an ink film on the substrate.

SOLVENT RECOVERY SYSTEM A system designed to remove evaporated solvents from dryer exhaust air and the pressroom air, collecting the solvent for reuse.

SPLICE/SPLICING The joining of the ends of rolled material.

SPLICING UNIT The mechanical section of the press that automatically splices the expiring roll of substrate to a new roll. Most commonly found on presses built to print board.

STATIC BALANCE A state of balance in a cylinder that involves only the weight of the cylinder. The weight of the cylinder is evenly distributed around all cross-sections of the cylinder.

SUPERCALENDER A process employing coiled iron rolls and cotton-filled rolls in combination with a steam shower to increase density, smoothness and gloss of paper.

THERMAL OXIDATION Incineration, usually used as part of a solvent recovery system.

THIXOTROPY A property of a liquid or plastic material that involves a reversible decrease of viscosity as the material is agitated or worked.

UV COATING Rapid drying coatings containing monomers, which respond to ultraviolet light exposure

VISCOSITY A fluid's resistance to flow, varying with temperature, agitation or rate of flow.

VOLATILE AIR COMPOUND (VOC) An air compound that has the property to readily vaporize at a relatively low temperature.

WEB GUIDE Device that keeps the web traveling straight or true through the press.

WIPING ANGLE Also called the set angle, the angle the doctor blade is set from the center line of the cylinder, before pressure is applied.

INDEX

ABOUT THE AUTHOR

Cheryl L. Kasunich is the executive vice president of the Gravure Association of America, a position she has held since 1992. Since 1978 she has been employed in the gravure industry, holding positions in purchasing and materials management, production management, environmental compliance, product development, marketing, and sales. A native of Pittsburgh, she received her Bachelor of Science degree from the University of Pittsburgh and has pursued graduate studies in human resource management and public management. She has taught purchasing and materials management for Duquesne University and Penn State University. Kasunich is the publisher and co-author of the textbook *Gravure: Process and Technology* as well as numerous publications on gravure technology and purchasing and materials management.

ABOUT GATF

The Graphic Arts Technical Foundation is a nonprofit, scientific, technical, and educational organization dedicated to the advancement of the graphic communications industries worldwide. Its mission is to serve the field as the leading resource for technical information and services through research and education.

For 74 years the Foundation has developed leading edge technologies and practices for printing. GATF's staff of researchers, educators, and technical specialists partner with nearly 2,000 corporate members in over 65 countries to help them maintain their competitive edge by increasing productivity, print quality, process control, and environmental compliance, and by implementing new techniques and technologies. Through conferences, satellite symposia, workshops, consulting, technical support, laboratory services, and publications, GATF strives to advance a global graphic communications community.

The Foundation publishes books on nearly every aspect of the field; learning modules (step-by-step instruction booklets); audiovisuals (CD-ROMs, videocassettes, slides, and audiocassettes); and research and technology reports. It also publishes *GATFWorld*, a bimonthly magazine of technical articles, industry news, and reviews of specific products.

For detailed information about GATF products and services, please visit our website at *http://www.gatf.org* or write to us at 200 Deer Run Road, Sewickley, PA 15143-2600. Phone: 412/741-6860.